Bonnie Weiss and Jay Earley have create
works using the IFS method. They show
and the parts that judge ourselves and others. Since John Bradshaw's work, we have become familiar with our inner child; Voice Dialogue helped us make friends with our inner critic. But this was just the beginning of exploring myself; Weiss and Earley have taken it to a whole new level. Their books, classes and workshops have helped myself and others to love ourselves using IFS's kind and gentle philosophy and method. It has been informative, entertaining, and fun to get to know my inner critic and discover that it actually has my best interests at heart.

—Eleanor Karn, artist, writer, lawyer, meditator, Walnut Creek, CA

Jay Earley and Bonnie Weiss's remarkable book will lead you beyond survival and old adaptations and into a life free from the confines of the past. Our Inner Critics are, after all, a way of protecting our inner exiles from further pain, suffering, humiliation and shame. This Critic book shows the path of transforming our Critics to have new roles in our psyche. *Self Therapy for Your Inner Critic* and it's companion volume, *Self-Therapy,* could be called the New Bible of Self-Transformation. They give a detailed map to support you in unfolding an adventure of healing—allowing for your flowering, fullness, and joy in living.

—Paula Smith-Hamilton, LCSW, PhD, Davis, CA

Reading *Self-Therapy for Your Inner Critic* has been a treat! As a pastor and a psychoanalyst who uses IFS more and more, I appreciate this book as a resource with enormous potential for healing in a place where so many people suffer—the assaults of their Inner Critic. Its clarity about the different types of Critics was edifying, and the exercises were easy to practice. While reading the book, I was able to become more acquainted with my own Critic parts in a deepening way. Weiss and Earley have made an important contribution to the endeavor of refining the application of IFS to a wider audience. I look forward to using this material in both the therapy office and classroom.

—Ann M. Akers, M.Div, LP, NCPsyA, New York City

This valuable book describes a fresh way of working with our Inner Critics through the Internal Family Systems therapeutic approach. The authors explore the human tendency to repeatedly undermine and damage our self-esteem. Instead of treating the Inner Critic as pathological, they describe and illustrate a positive strategy for transforming it that will appeal to many people. I have found it extremely helpful, both personally and professionally.

—Esther S. Battle, Ph.D., Yellow Springs, OH

This book is the next step in applying Internal Family Systems therapy. It gives you an innovative approach to working with your Internal Critic, illustrated by sharply drawn vignettes and insightful exercises. You will learn in detail how to embrace your Internal Critic so that it becomes an ally in reweaving your internal landscape.

—Cathy G. Duke, psychotherapist, Atlanta, GA

Jay and Bonnie have done a tremendous job of not only demystifying the Inner Critic but also providing readers with powerful, accessible tools for transforming it into a positive force in the personality. Their work is a rich contribution to Internal Family Systems and an important source of healing for everyone fortunate enough to experience it.

—Kira Freed, M.A, IFS Life Coach, Tucson, AZ

This book goes way beyond previous works on the Inner Critic. Jay Earley and Bonnie Weiss provide coaches with an entire tool box of tests, forms, ideas, and techniques for setting clients free from the Inner Critic trap.

—Gary Goodwin, creativity coach, VA

Self-Therapy for Your Inner Critic

Transforming Self-Criticism into Self-Confidence

Foreword by James Flaherty

Jay Earley, PhD
and
Bonnie Weiss, LCSW

Pattern System Books
Larkspur, California

Pattern System Books
140 Marina Vista Ave.
Larkspur, CA 94939
415-924-5256
www.patternsystembooks.com

ISBN: 978-0-9843927-1-1
ISBN-10: 0-9843927-1-8
LCCN: 2010937308

Printed in the United States of America

Contents

Foreword

For everyone I know, including myself, the inner critic causes unnecessary suffering, smothers initiative, wreaks havoc in relationships, and defeats change efforts. It's easy to locate—simply pay attention when you try something new, prepare for an important activity, or get introduced to a potential date or employer, and the critic will show up in full force. Undoubtedly you know what I'm talking about.

Distinguishing the critic is an essential first step in being able to intervene in its awkward, painful interruptions of our plans, self-development, and interactions with others. This extraordinarily helpful book—using transcripts from real conversations, playful illustrations, checklists, and questionnaires—makes taking this first step a sure and accurate one for any reader.

What to do once we find the critic? Ah, there's the rub. Criticizing our critic doesn't help; giving in to it diminishes us; trying to fight with it tangles us up in endless struggle. Here's where the book's real power comes into play. The authors, both deeply experienced in Internal Family Systems Therapy, clearly show a step-by-step process of diminishing the critic's power and transforming it into an ally through psychological alchemy, which is at the heart of their therapeutic method. They've found the perfect balance point by writing a book that isn't too dense in theory to be useful and isn't too superficial to have much lasting impact.

The inner critic is often disguised, defended, and deeply enmeshed within us in contradictory thoughts, feelings, and sensations. In a further sign of the authors' true mastery of the topic, they make this confusing bundle of reactions clear and accessible.

The book also shows how we can gain access to parts of ourselves that can bring encouragement, continuous learning and self-correction to our most important activities and relationships. As a consequence, readers can develop themselves into someone with much greater confidence and independence of thought and action.

Please jump into this book and take on its activities, at first for yourself; they will bring you immediate relief and learning. Then, if you're someone who works with others, bring the book's practical wisdom to your clients. They will be grateful, well served, and left with much greater self-knowledge and competence.

With gratitude, respect, and admiration for Jay and Bonnie, I wholeheartedly recommend you bring your full commitment and dedication to this book.

James Flaherty
Founder of New Ventures West, Integral Coaching®
Author of *Coaching: Evoking Excellence in Others*

Acknowledgements

We are deeply grateful to Dick Schwartz for creating such a brilliant method of therapy, which makes it possible to profoundly change people's Inner Critics. We have learned so much about the human psyche and about the Inner Critic from our therapy clients, group members, and the students in our IFS and Inner Critic classes, as well as the participants in the IFS training programs we have helped to lead. We received additional help from those people who volunteered to read early versions of some of the chapters and provide feedback, and also those who were the guinea pigs for the first versions of the Inner Critic Questionnaire and Profile Program.

Stefanie Weiss helped us think through the early stages of the book and edited part of the manuscript. Kira Freed has done a thorough job of editing and proofreading the entire work. Marny Parkin has been a blessing with her skills of laying out the book's interior. Jeanenne Chase Langford's creative eye is always available to us and we loved working with her on book cover design. Ed Hinkelman and Gayle Madison helped us birth the ideas that led to our Inner Critic Questionnaire. We deeply appreciate the ongoing support and holding of our IFS community group. A special thanks to Joan Slater and Mindy Lamberson whose creative input supported the unfolding of this work.

Karen Donnelly has once again produced wonderful, evocative illustrations to bring the Inner Critics and Champions to life. We appreciate her Herculean efforts to fit us into her busy life. Marla Silverman has been the inexhaustible champion of this work. She has been there all the way through, reading every chapter, listening to new ideas, and providing feedback whenever we needed it. George Silverman suggested the great term "Inner Champion" for us to use.

Our virtual assistant, Doreen DeJesus, has been continually in the background helping with innumerable tasks. Kathy Wilber has done an excellent job on the programming for our Inner Critic Questionnaire and Profile Program. Riley Miller and Jaime Becker have focused their keen eyes on the project. Jay has learned a great deal about how to get the book into print from the generous participants in the Self-Publishing Listserv.

Introduction

The Birth of the Inner Champion

B*onnie writes*: Over the years, I have worked with hundreds of women on deeply personal issues related to self-esteem. These women sought counseling in an effort to have coherent, meaningful lives and to fulfill their potential for satisfaction and happiness. Four years ago, I was seeing a number of impressive women who were gifted with a variety of capacities—intellectual acuity, musical talent, personality, inner and outer beauty. Despite their many gifts, the common thread that kept jumping out at me was their self-doubt and self-hatred.

I imagined that if I could put these women in the same room—to see and reflect each other—they would sense their similar conundrum and be able to gain some perspective on it. As a therapist, I had helped people work with their "superego" for many years. However, for this group, the concept of the "Inner Critic" seemed more appropriate. They were constantly being harassed by a demeaning, critical voice. If they had a great job that used all their time and energy, they were criticized by an internal voice for not having a fabulous boyfriend. If they decided to stay home with their children, they were overcome with feelings of deficiency when their sisters had careers. Even if they were radiantly beautiful, they were never satisfied with their bodies. If they were bright and articulate, they were worried about their looks or professional standing.

I was struck by how the Inner Critic was so integrated into their cellular identity that, like white on rice, these women couldn't imagine that its castigations were not just the "plain, sad, simple truth" about them. I developed a passion to make a difference in their lives. I wanted to help them find an antidote to these nattering voices. The image that surfaced was an exuberant chorus of women's voices surrounding each one, saying words that took away the power of the Critic and freed them to love themselves. I wanted them to remember that self-esteem was their birthright. I set out to design a process the allowed each woman to separate from her Critic and find her own personal mantra of love, assurance, and support. With that, I decided to bring these women together in the first Women's Inner Critic Workshop in 2006.

As the workshop date drew closer, I had a difficult professional moment. I made a thoughtless comment that I believed had serious consequences for a client. As it turned out, my actions were not the cause of her difficulties, but there were a few weeks when I was being extremely hard on myself. I was on an airplane to New York, planning the workshop and, ironically, trying to quiet my own Inner Critic, a demonic Guilt Tripper.

The methods I had used in the past—confronting it, separating from it, or justifying myself to it—were not working. It felt as if I needed bigger guns—more power and capacity. I had an image of a personal guide who loved me and supported me. This guide, which is clearly an aspect of me, had the capacity to stand up to my Inner Critic, which gave me some emotional space so I could think and regain my center. The guide had the perspective to see the entirety of who I am, not just a moment of lapse. It was able to comfort and nurture the child part of me who was taking the brunt of the criticism. And it had the practical ability to develop a clear action plan to make sure my client was OK.

And so the idea of the Inner Champion was born. The Inner Champion can be developed and cultivated to be a vibrant resource in your psyche. It nurtures and cares for you, provides a wider vista of guidance, and helps you take charge of your inner life and actions.

The Evolution of Our Inner Critic Work

Over the past five years, we have each deepened our understanding of how the Inner Critic operates in people's psyches and the best ways to work with it. We had already been using Internal Family Systems Therapy (IFS), a very powerful form of therapy that works with subpersonalities, or *parts.* We each began to lead workshops and classes in which people learned to apply IFS to their struggles with the Inner Critic. As we observed our participants' inner process, we discovered that a whole cluster of parts arises in response to self-criticism. We learned how these parts relate to each other and the best ways to work with them to resolve this issue.

It has been a fun and exciting time for us, working so closely together on a project of this scope for the first time. It has prompted us to look more deeply at our own internal and external critics and has brought us even closer. We are now delighted to be bringing this work out into the wider world through this book as well as other means.

Chapter 1

You Aren't the Problem It's Your Inner Critic

People are like stained-glass windows:
They sparkle and shine when the sun is out
But when the darkness sets in,
their true beauty is revealed
only if there is a light from within.

—Elizabeth Kubler-Ross

Do you struggle with bouts of depression and low self-esteem? Do you feel ashamed or guilty or hopeless at times? Take heart—this book offers a solution. Based on a powerful form of psychotherapy, *Self-Therapy for Your Inner Critic* can help you put an end to your painful feelings and help you grow into the person you've always dreamed of being. The surprising and wonderful news is that many people can achieve this transformation *on their own,* without the intervention of a psychotherapist. It's time for your suffering to end because you *can* transform your life. Vibrant self-esteem is your birthright; you needn't settle for anything less.

Many of us go through periods of believing there is something inherently wrong with us. When we explore inside, we are shocked to find out that our low self-esteem isn't really valid. It comes from our *Inner Critic,* which is a major underlying cause of depression and shame. It's both a surprise and a relief to learn that your Inner Critic is responsible for your feelings of worthlessness. When you feel ashamed, hopeless, inadequate, or just plain awful about yourself, it's because your Inner Critic is attacking you. It has a variety of methods, but most commonly, it works by hammering you with negative messages about your self-worth. It may criticize your looks, your work habits, your intelligence, the way you care for others, or any number of other things.

Your Inner Critic may:

- Evaluate and judge your feelings and behavior and sometimes your core self.
- Tell you what you should and shouldn't do.
- Criticize you for not meeting its expectations or the expectations of people who are important to you.
- Doubt you and tell you that you can't be successful.
- Shame you for who you are.
- Make you feel guilty about things you have done.

These judgmental messages aren't valid. This book will show you how to refute them, integrate your Inner Critic, and reweave your internal landscape.

In addition to depression and low self-esteem, your Inner Critic can cause a myriad of other problems, such as performance fears, writer's block, self-doubt, shame, guilt, obsessive thinking, addiction, and more.

IFS and Your Inner Critic

This book is a companion to *Self-Therapy: A Step-by-Step Guide to Creating Wholeness and Healing Your Inner Child Using IFS,* which shows how to do IFS therapy on your own or with a partner. Internal Family Systems Therapy (IFS) is a new, cutting-edge form of psychotherapy developed by psychologist Richard Schwartz, which has been spreading rapidly across the country in the last decade. IFS is not only extremely effective with a wide variety of psychological issues, but it is also user-friendly and lends itself especially well to self-therapy. IFS makes it easy to comprehend the complexity of your psyche.

This book shows you how to apply IFS to transforming your Inner Critic. You will get more out of it if you have read *Self-Therapy* or if you are already familiar with IFS. In this book, you'll learn how to take each of the steps in the IFS process and use it to work effectively with Inner Critic parts. In fact, we reference the relevant sections of *Self-Therapy* as we go along. However, we explain the relevant IFS concepts and procedures as needed in this book, so you will be able to use it successfully even if you have no previous knowledge of IFS. If we use any term that is unfamiliar to you, look it up in the Glossary, Appendix A.

One important caveat: Although many people have tremendous success using our approach, others will see more progress with the additional support of a trained psychotherapist. (See **www.selfleadership.org** to find an IFS therapist.) If you are in the midst of a major life crisis, it's always a good idea to seek help. Regardless of whether you work with a practitioner, this book will help you proceed on your journey to self-love.

Because the Inner Critic is one of the most challenging issues people face, we have become fascinated with how to apply IFS to transforming it. We have developed a number of innovations that are the basis for this book. This approach can teach you how to relate to yourself with compassion and caring instead of anger and criticism. This will help your true, confident Self to shine through—the Self that isn't occluded by the negative messages of the Inner Critic. By going through this process, you reconnect with yourself and gain renewed focus, creativity, and self-confidence. The best part is that most people can do it on their own, and if you do need a therapist, IFS practitioners are available in most locations to help.

IFS recognizes that our psyches are made up of different *parts*, sometimes called *subpersonalities*. You can think of them as little people inside us. Each has its own perspective, feelings, memories, goals, and motivations. For example, one part of you might be trying to lose weight and another part might want to eat a lot. We all have parts like the abandoned child, the pleaser, the angry part, the loving caretaker, and, of course, the Inner Critic. IFS distinguishes between two primary types of parts. *Protectors* are parts that try to prevent us from being hurt and feeling pain. *Exiles* are parts that are in pain from childhood. (For more detail, see Chapters 1 and 2 of *Self-Therapy*.)

Let's see how the Inner Critic played out in one person's psyche.

Jeanette's Story

Jeanette had a bad case of low self-esteem. Even when she was a child, all her teachers were puzzled by this. She was smart and musically gifted but had absolutely no confidence. She never auditioned for the orchestra or for school plays even when she was encouraged to do so. As she got older and this pattern continued, she ended up holding minimal jobs that didn't come close to tapping her native talents. She just assumed that she wouldn't amount to anything. Every time she had an inclination to reach out and try something challenging, she experienced a sinking feeling in her chest and a grey cloud descended on her, so she gave up on the idea.

One afternoon Jeanette's friend Lynn was having a very bad day; she complained to Jeanette of heaviness in her heart. Lynn was talking about a critical voice that she heard inside of her. Suddenly something clicked with Jeanette; she realized that she recognized the voice her friend was describing. It lived inside her, too! It was saying critical things like: "You aren't any good. You can't do it. Don't even try." She had always just assumed that this was **the truth** about her. She had never viewed these harmful messages as coming from a separate part of her psyche. She recalled how she longed to try out for high school musicals but this other voice spoke so forcefully that she didn't dare.

This was Jeannette's Inner Critic. Since she hadn't been consciously aware of it until that moment, she had no way to communicate with it. She saw no way to confront the source of her negative beliefs about herself.

Jeannette's Inner Critic

When Jeanette became aware of how her Critic was tearing her down and ruining her life, her natural response was to get angry at it and want to get rid of it. If she had turned to conventional therapy, she might have been encouraged to overcome it. She would have seen it as the enemy. However this approach wouldn't have been very effective because when we battle with the Inner Critic, it just becomes more entrenched.

Jeanette started IFS therapy with Bonnie, exploring her psyche and gradually getting to know her Inner Critic.[1] To her amazement, she discovered that this part was actually trying to *help* her. Even though it was causing hopelessness and depression, it was doing this in a distorted attempt to protect her. The Inner Critic is an

1. See Chapters 4–8 in *Self-Therapy*.

IFS *protector.* It wanted to keep her safe from failure and humiliation, and it figured that the best way to do so was to prevent her from ever trying anything difficult. It accomplished this by constantly judging and discouraging her.

Jeannette's Inner Critic and Criticized Child

Once Jeanette realized that her Critic was trying to help her, her anger melted and she began to understand it and treat it more kindly. (In IFS, you never have to fight with a part or try to get rid of it. You can gradually develop a trusting relationship with it and help it to relate to you more constructively.) As Jeanette developed a friendlier attitude toward her Critic, it became more reasonable and was willing to negotiate about the best way to protect her.

Exploring further, Jeanette discovered another part of her that received the negative messages from the Critic. This was a young child part who believed these judgments and felt worthless, defeated, and hopeless. We call this part the *Criticized Child.*

It is an IFS *exile.* Jeanette learned that she could also relate to this part. She befriended it from a place of love and compassion.

Then, using the IFS procedure, she accessed those childhood memories that were the origin of her Inner Critic,[2] memories of being judged and dismissed and made to feel worthless. The Criticized Child is the exiled part who was hurt by those judgments. Jeanette then healed this Child through her love and helped it to release its feelings of shame and worthlessness. Her Critic then receded into the background and caused less trouble in her life.

Jeannette's Inner Champion

2. See Chapters 10–12 in *Self-Therapy.*

In addition, as a result of this work, Jeanette discovered a helpful aspect of herself, one that we call the *Inner Champion*. It has the capacity to support and encourage us in the face of Inner Critic attacks. Jeanette was able to develop and strengthen this caring Champion which only wanted the best for her. It told her that she had a lot of talent and could accomplish great things in the world. She learned to evoke it when necessary and take in its support.

Her Champion said, "You are OK just the way you are. You can do it. I'm proud of you." This helped Jeanette to take the risk to develop her musical talent and go to auditions. At long last, she moved ahead professionally in a career that she really loved. As her Inner Champion took over for her Inner Critic, she became happier and self-confident enough to pursue her dreams.

Responses to the Critic That Don't Work Well

Ignore It and Think Positively

Once you become aware of the problems your Inner Critic is causing, you might try to just ignore its attacks and think positive thoughts about yourself. This is, of course, much better than simply believing your Critic, but it won't solve the problem because you're not really dealing with the Critic. This tactic may work at times, but then your Critic will override your attempts to ignore it and may sneer at your positive thoughts. Or it may sneak up on you with subtle attacks that you don't even notice.

Argue with It

You might try to convince the Critic that it is wrong and that you are really worthwhile, competent, smart, and so on. This is better than the previous strategy, but it still gives away your power. The Critic may or may not be convinced. And even though you may win the argument at times, your Critic usually comes back with even more powerful attacks.

Banish It

Another obvious strategy is to try to get rid of your Critic—to give it the old heave-ho. Unfortunately, this really isn't possible. First of all, you can't get rid of a part of your psyche any more than you can get ride of a part of your body. You won't be able to cast out or banish your Inner Critic forever. It might go underground for a while, but it will pop up later and cause you even more grief.

Second, your Inner Critic is actually trying to help you, in its own distorted, confused way. Once you explore your Critic in a deeper way, you'll come to understand why your Critic is attacking you, and you'll see, just as Jeanette did, that it does have your best interests at heart, as surprising as that may sound. Your Inner Critic may be negative and harsh, but just like any IFS protector, its function is to protect you from pain. This means that you can connect with it and develop a cooperative relationship with it, which will help to transform it into a valuable resource instead of a problem.

Many approaches to the Inner Critic view it as just an attacking bully and try to get rid of it. They miss the larger understanding from IFS that *all* our parts are trying to help us. When you accept and work with all your parts, including the Critic, none are demonized, and this leads to wholeness and your highest potential.

One important thing to remember about parts is that they usually only know one way to act and react. This is because they come from our childhood, when our psyches were still developing and we were faced with dangerous situations that we were too young to handle well. Our parts did the best they could, often using strategies that were extreme and shortsighted. Parts are not necessarily flexible, rational, or mature. (This is especially true in the case of the Inner Critic. All it knows how to do is judge; whether or not that works.)

What You Can Get from This Book

We have identified seven types of Inner Critics. You can take a questionnaire to determine which ones are problematic for you. This will give you a better grasp of how to work with them.

This book shows in detail how to work with your Inner Critic using IFS, how to heal the pain of your Criticized Child, and how to help your Critic to let go of its judgmental role and become an ally in your life. You will also learn how to awaken your Inner Champion to support your self-esteem and your right to be yourself, and to encourage you to take the steps to create the life you want.

You aren't stuck with the anguish and difficulties that stem from your Inner Critic. Your inner world can change, helping you to feel confident and capable, and allowing your life's journey to unfold in an exciting, self-directed way.

In the next chapter, we'll begin the journey by looking at the seven types of Critics and how they are trying to help you.

Chapter 2

The Seven Types of Inner Critics

The world is nothing but my perception of it.
I see only through myself.
I hear only through the filter of my story.

—Byron Katie

There isn't just one Inner Critic part. Most people have a number of self-judging protectors that operate in different ways. For example, you might have one Critic that attacks you for how you overeat and how much you weigh, and another Critic that tells you that you're lazy and should be working harder. These are most likely different parts, and you will need to work with each one separately.

Furthermore, there are a variety of Critic parts that operate in different ways. We have identified seven types of Critics, each of which has a different motivation and strategy. These can be quite useful as a way of learning about the possibilities for your Critics; however, don't take them as hard-and-fast descriptions of your parts. Which ones do you recognize within yourself?

Perfectionist

The Perfectionist tries to get you to do everything perfectly. This part has very high standards for behavior, performance, and production. When you don't meet its standards, the Perfectionist attacks you by saying that your work or behavior isn't good enough. This makes it hard to finish projects. Sometimes the Perfectionist even makes it difficult to get started, as with writer's block. Our

Perfectionist

clients with Perfectionist Critics have seen them as a crab with pincers, a schoolmarm with super-high standards, a magnifying glass, and an inspector, especially El Exigente, "the demanding one," from a 1970s coffee commercial.

Inner Controller

The Inner Controller tries to control impulsive behavior, such as overeating, getting enraged, using drugs, or other addictions. It shames you after you binge or use. It is usually in a constant battle

Inner Controller

with an impulsive part. Our clients with Inner Controllers have seen them as a bulldog, a lion tamer, an angry guard, or a shaming mother.

Taskmaster

The Taskmaster tries to get you to work hard in order to be successful. It attacks you and tells you that you're lazy, stupid, or

Taskmaster

incompetent in an attempt to motivate you. It often gets into a battle with a part that procrastinates as a way of avoiding work. The Taskmaster might be seen as a demanding foreman, A vigilant watchdog, a boot in the center of your back, or someone constantly keeping a bunch of plates spinning.

Underminer

The Underminer tries to undermine your self-confidence and self-esteem so you won't take risks that might end in failure. It tells you that you are worthless and inadequate, and that you'll never amount to anything. It may also try to prevent you from getting too big, powerful, or visible in order to avoid the threat of attack and rejection. (Jeannette's Critic was an Underminer.) The experience of being undermined can feel like having the rug pulled out from under you, walking on a treadmill where you work and sweat

Underminer

but go nowhere, having a rope tied to your middle so you can't go forward, or coming up against a glass wall.

Destroyer

Destroyer

The Destroyer makes pervasive attacks on your fundamental self-worth. It is deeply shaming and tells you that you shouldn't exist. It can be experienced as a crushing force that wipes out your vitality or a pervasive negative energy that stamps out any sign of creativity, spontaneity, or desire. It might look like Darth Vader, a giant spider, a leech on the back of the neck, or an elephant crushing you underfoot.

Guilt Tripper

The Guilt Tripper attacks you for a specific action you took (or didn't take) in the past that was harmful to someone, especially someone you care about. This Critic might also attack you for violating a deeply held value. It constantly makes you feel bad and will never forgive you. It might also make you feel guilty for repeated behaviors that it considers unacceptable in an attempt to get you to stop. Images of the Guilt Tripper from our clients include a nun,

Guilt Tripper

a judge, a despot exiling someone, a black cloud descending, or a weight on the shoulders. It can make you feel oozy and icky, heavy in the chest, or as if you are being smashed with a huge hammer.

Molder

The Molder tries to get you to fit a certain societal mold or act in a certain way that is based on your family or cultural mores. This can be any kind of mold, for example, caring, aggressive, outgoing, intellectual, or polite. This Critic attacks you when you don't fit

Molder

and praises you when you do. Images for the Molder include a prison guard, a cage, a straightjacket, or a large rule book, like a holy text, that determines what you should do at every moment.

Even though we are using these seven categories of Critics, remember that each of your parts is unique. Please call your parts by whatever name seems right; don't feel as though you must use Taskmaster or Underminer. Each of your Critics will have its own unique characteristics. For example, your Perfectionist won't be the same as anyone else's, and you might have one Critic that has characteristics of both a Molder and Guilt Tripper, for example. You might even have a part that has some characteristics of a Critic and some other qualities that are not Critic-like. Don't pigeon-hole your parts according to our descriptions of these categories. Discover your own parts and their unique attributes.

Examples of Inner Critics

Let's look at some common examples of the ways Inner Critic messages manifest in our lives. You may recognize yourself in some of these scenarios.

Jill had an important date planned with someone she really liked. The night before the date, she started to feel nervous and ran to the fridge, binging on chocolate cake. Right after she wiped away the crumbs, she looked in the mirror and heard her Critic saying, "You look fat!" and "No man will ever marry you!" She suddenly felt uglier than she ever had in her life. She worried furiously about how she was going to look even though it was still twenty-four hours before her date. When the time for the date finally arrived, she was so nervous and agitated that she could barely communicate. Jill was thus *less* like her authentic self on the date and ended up sabotaging her chances of making a good impression. Jill's Critic is an **Inner Controller** because it tried to stop her from overeating.

Charlie was halfway through an important project when his Inner Critic showed up while he was sitting in front of his computer. It told him that that the work he'd done so far was "garbage" and then made him check and recheck it, wasting his precious time. Under this degree of pressure, the rest of the project ended up being late. If his Inner Critic hadn't derailed his work in this way, Charlie might have done a stellar job and gotten big kudos from his boss. Charlie's Inner Critic is a **Perfectionist.**

Jennifer is the mother of a ten-year-old boy named Sean. Sean was not meeting academic standards, but Jennifer felt as though she herself was failing. She had a job outside of the house and believed that her inability to spend every afternoon with Sean was at the root of his problems at school. When he brought home his report card, Jennifer acted outwardly nurturing and caring, but on the inside she was crying, thinking it was her fault. Her Critic said, "It's your fault! You haven't helped him enough." Jennifer's Inner Critic is a **Guilt Tripper.**

Exercise: Which Critics Do You Have?

Think of a way that one of your Critic parts attacks you. Under what circumstances does it do this?

____

What does it say to you?

____

____

____

____

____

Which of these seven types of Critics do you think it is?

____

In order to allow you to more easily write out the answers to this exercise and all the others in the book, we have created a Companion Workbook that you can download for free from our website **www.personal-growth-programs.com.**

Example

Here is how Lisa filled out the sheet for this exercise:

Think of a way that one of your Critic parts attacks you. Under what circumstances does it do this?

Whenever I eat too much.

What does it say to you?

You're a fat slob.

No man will every be interested in you.

You should be ashamed of yourself for pigging out like that.

Which of these seven types of Critics do you think it is?

Inner Controller

The Inner Critic Questionnaire

We have devised a questionnaire to help you determine which of the seven types of Critics are a problem for you. It is short and easy, usually not taking more than 5 or 6 minutes. The easiest way to take it is on our website **www.psychemaps.com**. You can also take it here.

Answer each of the following questions with a number that corresponds to the following:

0 =Never 1=Not often 2=Occasionally 3=Frequently 4=Always

Write your answer in the blank

Q1 __ I feel like I am intrinsically flawed.

Q2 __ I set high standards for myself.

Q3 __ I feel terrible about myself when I get out of control.

Q4 __ I push myself to work very hard so I can achieve my goals.

Q5 __ When I think of trying something new and challenging, I give up before I begin.

Q6 __ I am ashamed of everything about myself.

Q7 __ I am troubled by something I have done that I cannot forgive myself for.

Q8 __ I know who I ought to be, and I'm hard on myself when I act differently.

Q9 __ I expend a great deal of effort trying to control my impulsive behavior.

Q10 __ My self-confidence is so low that I don't believe I can succeed at anything.

Q11 __ I attack myself when I make a mistake.

Q12 __ I have trouble holding onto a positive sense of myself.

Q13 __ I have a hard time feeling OK about myself when I'm not acting in accordance with my childhood programming.

Q14 __ There is no end to the things I have to do.

Q15 __ I do things to people that I feel terribly guilty for.

Q16 __ There are indulgent parts of me that take over and get me into trouble, and then I punish myself for it.

Q17 __ I believe that it is safer not to try than to fail.

Q18 __ I get anxious and self-critical when things don't come out just right.

Q19 __ I feel ashamed when I don't measure up to others' expectations.

Q20 __ I tell myself that, if I were a good person, I would take better care of people I care about.

Q21 __ At a deep level I feel like I don't have the right to exist.

Q22 __ I feel bad because I am too lazy to really make it in the world.

Q23 __ I feel really ashamed of some of my habits.

Q24 __ I spend much more time than is needed on a project in order to make it as good as possible.

Q25 __ I have a nagging feeling that I am bad.

Q26 __ I try really hard to overcome my tendency to avoid doing tasks.

Q27 __ I feel bad because I can't be what my family or culture expects of me.

Q28 __ I feel that I don't have what it takes to succeed.

Now fill in your numerical answers from above in the blanks below and add up each line to get a total score for each group of four questions. This gives you a numerical score from 0 to 16 for each of the seven types of Critics.

Q2 __ + Q11 __ + Q18 __ + Q24 __ = __ Perfectionist Score

Q3 __ + Q9 __ + Q16 __ + Q23 __ = __ Inner Controller Score

Q4 __ + Q14 __ + Q22 __ + Q26 __ = __ Taskmaster Score

Q5 __ + Q10 __ + Q17 __ + Q28 __ = __ Underminer Score

Q1 __ + Q6 __ + Q12 __ + Q21 __ = __ Destroyer Score

Q7 __ + Q15 __ + Q20 __ + Q25 __ = __ Guilt Tripper Score

Q8 __ + Q13 __ + Q19 __ + Q27 __ = __ Molder Score

If you scored 9 or higher for a Critic, there is a good chance that it is causing you problems. Those for which you scored 7 or 8 might be problematic. Those with 7 or less are less likely to be.

The Inner Critic as Enforcer

One of the main reasons our Inner Critic parts judge us is to enforce a certain way of being—perfect, hardworking, moderate, or cautious, for example. If a Taskmaster Critic always thinks it is important for you to have your nose to the proverbial grindstone, it will push you to overwork and attack you when you don't. However, if you are generally a conscientious, focused worker, then there is no need for a Taskmaster Critic. You might very well have a part of you that works very hard, perhaps even too hard, but it wouldn't be a Critic, just a "hardworking" part.

Jay writes: This has the been the case with me. I have two hardworking parts, which I call the Achiever and the Accomplisher. The Achiever wants me to be highly successful professionally and tends to work very hard to get there, in a way that hasn't always been good for me. It isn't a Critic, however, because it has never judged me or pushed me. It just works hard. My Accomplisher is similar. It is ruled by my to-do list and gets completely caught up in getting things done, so that it can become like a machine with little presence or pleasure. But it isn't a Critic. It doesn't tell me to get things done. It just does them. I have worked on these parts for years, and now they have relaxed quite a bit. I am no longer driven to strive and can work with ease, which allows me a great deal of joy.

For any of the seven Critics, you might have a part that follows the rules so there is no need for the Critic to enforce them. For example, if have a Dieter Part that is very careful about the food you eat, there would be no need for an Inner Controller Critic to attack you. The Dieter might be overly rigid, but if it doesn't judge your eating, it's not a Critic.

This distinction highlights a very interesting characteristic of Inner Critic parts. *They have no power to act.* Therefore they must judge us and push us in an attempt to enforce the way they want us to act. If they had the power to act, they would just do it; they wouldn't have to criticize us. Isn't it interesting that Critics that we think are so powerful actually can't take action in the world? They certainly have the power to hurt us, and consequently they seem very powerful, but their judgments derive from their lack of power—from their frustration at not being able to act and their difficulty in getting us to act the way they want.

Because of the enforcer nature of Critics, one might suddenly judging you when you make a change in your life. Suppose you have been very careful about food all your adult life and have therefore never gotten any flak about your eating from a Critic. Lately you have been working on loosening up in some areas where you have felt restricted and are beginning to experiment with being more relaxed and less rigid about food. You might begin to be attacked by an Inner Controller Critic about this. Up until now, it didn't need to judge you because you were behaving in the way it wanted. Now that you are changing, it has become activated in order to enforce its view of how you should be.

The Criticized Child

Whenever we are being attacked or judged by an Inner Critic part, there is always a second part of us that is receiving this attack and feeling hurt, depressed, or worthless. We call this part the *Criticized Child.* This is an exile who believes the attack and feels ashamed or guilty, bad, or inadequate. Many people, at first, don't make a distinction between the Critic and the Criticized Child, but doing so is crucial to unraveling this difficult issue.

There are always two parts involved. One part attacks us, and a second part feels attacked. For example, suppose your Critic sneers at you and tells you that you're so shy that you're a loser and no one likes you. The sneering Critic feels harsh, judgmental, and dismissive toward you. There is a second part of you (the Criticized Child) that believes this attack and feels rejected, ashamed, and worthless. You will need to work with both parts, but in very different ways.

There are usually more than two parts involved with the Inner Critic, in fact, a whole cluster of parts. We will be introducing more of them in each chapter, and developing a graphic representation of this cluster. Here is a beginning view of this cluster:

Inner Critic Cluster

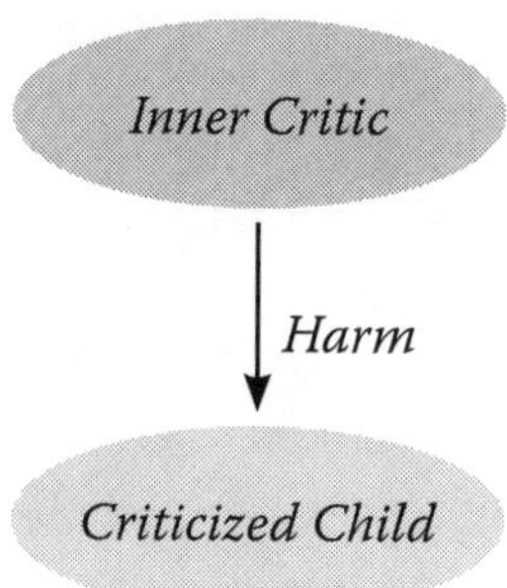

Summary

In this chapter, you learned about the seven types of Critics and got a sense of which ones are problematic for you. You also learned about the difference between your Inner Critic and your Criticized Child. In the next chapter, we will look at how gender affects Inner Critic judgments.

Chapter 3

Gender and the Inner Critic

The first problem for all of us, men and women, is not to learn, but to unlearn.

—*Gloria Steinem*

Our Inner Critic messages are strongly influenced by a host of cultural factors—gender, race, religion, ethnicity, sexual orientation, socioeconomic class, and so on. Women's Inner Critics, for example, are more likely to judge them about their bodies and sexual attractiveness, while men's tend to judge them about their worldly success. People who break away from the religion or national identity of their childhood will often have an Inner Critic that judges them for that transgression and attempts to bring them back into the fold. People of color and various sexual orientations often have to cope with Critics that echo society's prejudices.

Hal and Sidra Stone, in their book *Embracing Your Inner Critic,* talk about the Inner Patriarchy as a "powerful ally of the Inner Critic in women." They define the Inner Patriarch as "the inner representation of the outer societal beliefs in the inferiority of women, and it echoes all the judgments of women that are prevalent in our culture."[1]

1. Hal and Sidra Stone, *Embracing Your Inner Critic,* Harper San Francisco, 1993, p. 93.

They believe that women suffer more acutely than men from Inner Critic issues as a result of years of patriarchal thinking. Women believe they need to "improve" and please others just to level the playing field.

Two-and-a-half times as many women as men have taken our Inner Critic questionnaire, confirming the Stones' experience that more women than men consciously struggle with their Inner Critics. Of the respondents, women rated their difficulties with their Critics slightly higher than men for all seven types, and more so for the Molder and Underminer Critics. These are just preliminary findings; we will be studying further how people's Critics are distributed over the seven types.

Changes in Gender Attitudes

We won't try to cover much of the broad scope of sociocultural issues in this short chapter; we will mainly focus on our knowledge of how recent changes in attitudes about gender have affected the content of Inner Critic attacks in the populations we are familiar with.

The revolution in gender roles over the past 40 years has blasted open expectations for many men and women. We have noticed that our clients, our friends, and ourselves see brand-new vistas of our potentials. Our deeply held beliefs about the roles we can play and the satisfactions we are allowed have been challenged. Many women can now see themselves exerting their strength and influence in previously unimagined arenas—career ambition, professional position, corporate management, political influence, activist and nonprofit leadership, and media visibility. They are now allowed to tap into their desire for authority and power without being ashamed of exerting leadership and showing competence.

Many men, on the other hand, are interested in being more personally open, communicative, and in touch with their feelings, or they are being challenged to be that way by their partners. Men with families are now asked to be responsible on the home front—sharing child-care responsibilities, being on the food-prep rotation, and being attentive to their partner's emotional needs. Today, a young married couple might take for granted that the man may leave work early to pick up the kids so the woman can work late or make a big presentation to a client in another city.

Man and Woman juggling responsibilities

Bonnie's Story

The type of Critic I have struggled with most is the Guilt Tripper. I come by it naturally because of my Jewish heritage. It judges me for not being enough, not for lacking capacity, but for not being fully present and attentive. If I am focused on one thing—my work, my garden, my spiritual development, my current craft project—there is always something I am neglecting.

I am a woman of the '60s generation, whose possibilities exploded out of the women's movement. The emotional challenge of that time for me was to balance the excitement of a real career with the desire to be a wife and mother—and then a successful single mom. Whenever I focused on one of those options, I felt that I should be attending to the other. When I was working, I felt as though I should be with my daughter, and when I was with her, there were career tasks and stimulating challenges that distracted me. I was pulled by travel and the exploration of spiritual issues, which opened and deepened me but did not settle me down during those years.

My Guilt Tripper manifests in a pair of regular dreams, one usually following the other. In the first dream, I am about to graduate from college, and I realize that I have not finished a Civics course. All term I have been meaning to talk to the professor but haven't gotten around to it. On the day of the final, I realize, to my great dismay, that I don't even know where the classroom is. I feel foolish and guilty that I have not taken care of this responsibility properly.

In the second dream, I am walking the streets of New York City with my beautiful five-year-old daughter. She is carrying a box of jewelry with chains dribbling out the sides. I decide to leave her with a group of strangers in order to go to an important meeting. Halfway there, on the subway, I think, *Maybe that wasn't such a great idea.* I feel guilty about not paying proper attention to my role as a parent.

Women

Bonnie writes: Expanded roles for many women I know have brought with them conflicting expectations, both internal and external. Now there is a whole smorgasbord of things that we can feel lacking in. Before, we were limited to having a clean house; perfect children; a sexy body; a patient, supportive attitude toward our husbands; and the best cake at the bake sale. The sad story is that those expectations haven't really gone away. Added to them are having a career that brings in a substantial income, being facile with new technology, being up to date on current events, and making intelligent conversation with colleagues.

We now have an increasing abundance of reasons to put ourselves down and more arenas in which our Inner Critics may judge us. When focusing our attention on one of these areas, we often feel guilty that our scorecard is below par in another. We can drive ourselves shamelessly in one arena, egged on by a Perfectionist Critic that compares us to our sisters and always finds someone who is doing more, doing it easier, or looking better while doing it! We have many things higher on the priority list than ourselves and therefore must find ways to keep our basic needs in check. An Inner Critic attack is one great way to do this; it makes us feel small and unworthy.

The conflicting internal struggle about whether to put one's self out in the world is heightened by the plethora of possibilities. It is harder to hide behind that proverbial white picket fence and say, "I'm just a mom." We can no longer say, "I'm just a woman. I don't know things like that." Everyone knows that we could be doing more. Oprah is on every day at 4:00 to remind us. There are no more excuses. This triggers the part of us that fears that we are inadequate little girls going off to work in the big world in Mommy's clothing, and it activates an Underminer Critic that says we'll never be good enough.

It is my hope that identifying the seven types of Inner Critics will contribute to women being able to get space from self-judgment and experience a new kind of liberation.

Men

Jay writes: Many men I know also have new things to struggle with. Our avenues for deficiency and vulnerability to attack have also expanded. Now we may be expected to be aware of home and family issues, open in love relationships, and good in bed. These are new areas for Inner Critic attacks. Those men with young families may have to know the soccer schedule and the names of all their children's teachers. They may need to manage their careers while being more on call for schedule shifts.

Meanwhile, the old places of vulnerability to self-judgment are as prevalent as ever. Men are still expected to be successful, worldly, confident, masculine, powerful, and wealthy. And there is often an Inner Critic just waiting to judge us if we fall down in any of these areas—or worse yet, a Critic that constantly attacks us for never being adequate.

Summary

In this chapter, we looked briefly at how Inner Critics are affected by gender and how the gender revolution has affected our Critics. In the next chapter, you will learn how to begin to work successfully with your Critic.

Chapter 4

Your Critic Isn't as Powerful and Frightening as You Think

As we tune into the Inner Critic, we begin to perceive it as an alarm system that signals a call for help. Someone is dialing 911. Someone is alerting us to the possibility of pain, shame or abandonment. It is as though the Inner Critic cries, "Look out! Please help me because I can't handle the situation."

—Hal and Sidra Stone,
Embracing Your Inner Critic

Your Critic's Positive Intent

One of the most shocking discoveries about our Inner Critics is that they are actually trying to help us. This is an amazing, powerful secret. An Inner Critic is an IFS protector. It is trying win approval from others or protect us from pain. As strange as it may seem, we have found this to be true over and over with hundreds of clients, and so have other IFS therapists.

Your Inner Critic has learned a strategy for helping you. It thinks that pushing and judging you will protect you from hurt and pain. It thinks that if it can get you to be a certain way—perfect, successful, cautious, nice, slim, outgoing, intellectual, macho, and so on—then you won't be shamed or rejected and you might even get approval from people who are important to you. It tries to get you to fit in by prescribing rules and then attacking you if you violate them. Sadly, attacking you actually backfires and causes you more suffering.

Nevertheless your Inner Critic is doing what it thinks is best for you, so you don't have to fight with it or overcome it. You don't have to win a battle; you don't have to get rid of it. You can discover what it thinks it's doing for you and make a positive connection with it. You can offer it appreciation for its efforts, and it can begin to trust you. Knowing that your Critic's heart is in the right place makes it possible to create a cooperative relationship with it. This makes an enormous difference in your internal landscape and sets the stage for deeper healing.

The Intimidating Critic

Many Inner Critic parts think they must be powerful and scary to do their job. They think they must dominate you and be in control of you to protect you, so they act tough and project power. But these parts are actually not as confident as they seem; they are scared about what might happen if they didn't do their job. Recall in *The Wizard of Oz* when Dorothy and her friends went to see the wizard, the Great and Terrible Oz, they saw a variety of images that were formidable and frightening. However, these were all just projected by a little man behind a screen to make himself seem powerful. He didn't actually have any magical powers at all. That is the way it often is with our Inner Critics. They are projections on the screens of our minds.

In fact, many Inner Critics are actually child parts that took on the burden of protecting you when you were young. You may have been in a dangerous situation in your family where you were being judged, harmed, or rejected, so a child part felt that something had to be done to protect you. This part believed that the only way to protect you was to judge you to try to shape you into becoming what your family wanted. It thought this was the way to stop you from being hurt, so it puffed itself up and began to attack you.

This child part isn't innately a nasty Critic. It started out with more noble characteristics—such as clarity, strength, assertiveness, or energy—before it took on this judgmental role. When it is able to let go of its attacking strategy, using the methods in this book, then it can regain its natural healthy role in your psyche.

Sarah's Attacker Critic

Let's look at a detailed example that illustrates the history of a Critic part. Sarah, a member of one of Jay's groups, was very frightened of her Inner Critic. It screamed and yelled at her and crushed her with its attacks and its power. It told her that she was worthless and would never amount to anything. She called her Critic the Attacker and visualized it as a huge, powerful monster that was attacking her physically; it had great muscles and a loud voice.

However, once she became openly interested in getting to know the Attacker, she discovered its positive intent. Here is what the Attacker said to her: "Attacking is a game in our family. They're all doing it, so I've got to do it, too, and I've got to be good at it. If they're going to do that to me, then I'm going to do it to myself so they can't do it to me worse. This gives me the power of not being hurt by them. I'm trying to protect this child part from being hurt by them and from feeling all that hate and criticism from the family. That's too painful, so if I hurt her (the Child part) instead, it won't be so bad because I'm the one hurting her—not the people that she really wants the love from."

After hearing this, Sarah's view of the Attacker gradually changed. And the Attacker itself also changed. It became visibly smaller, less threatening, and more reasonable.

Sarah's View of the Attacker Changes

The Attacker is dialoguing with Sarah

This is the part of the session that followed with Jay and Sarah.

Sarah: It's very competitive. The whole of my family is very competitive. The Attacker is doing two things: it's going to protect me from them, but it also wants to be the best. It's really sad that it has to do that to protect me from the family. I feel compassion for the Attacker that it had to do that.

Jay: So let the Attacker know of your compassion for it in some way. And see how it's responding to you.

This process helps to build the relationship between Sarah and the Attacker.

S: It's having trouble taking that in.

J: Ask what the trouble is. What makes it hard for the Attacker to take that in?

S: Because it's so caught up in having to fight to survive ... and to be heard.

J: So it's afraid that taking in your compassion will take the fight out of it?

S: Yeah, otherwise it'd get crushed by everyone in the family. It had to defend itself. That's why it attacks so much—because everybody else was better at attacking. Maybe it attacked my brother sometimes, but it certainly couldn't attack my mom or dad.

J: I see. So it ended up attacking you because it could do that.

S: Yeah. But it did that to protect me from them. "I'll do it to myself so they don't hurt me." That's what it was about, yeah. "Anything you do can't get to me because I've hurt myself first."

J: It sounds as if you really understand where the Attacker got that strategy from.

S: It's crazy isn't it? But it made sense at the time, it's all that part could do.

J: Let it know that you really understand where it was coming from.

S: OK.

J: Check and see how the Attacker is responding to you now.

S: It's calming down a bit.

J: See if there's anything more the Attacker wants to show you about what happened to make it take on this role.

S: We've pretty much got it. It thanks you for being patient enough to let it get this out.

The Attacker now seems to trust Sarah and me, so I go on to see if it will give us permission to heal the exile it is protecting.

J: Good. So it did all this to try to protect this exile that's been so attacked in your family. See if it would be willing to give you permission to work with that exile.

S: It's scared.

J: That's understandable. Ask it what its scared of.

S: That this Scared Kid would have to feel all that hate and criticism from the family. It's trying to protect that exile, it doesn't want the Scared Kid to feel that pain.

J: That's really understandable. It's great that it wants to protect the Scared Kid. So let the Attacker know that the Scared Kid is already feeling that pain.

The Attacker thinks that if it gives permission to work with the Scared Kid, that will cause the exile to feel its childhood pain. However, exiles are already *in pain. They have been holding that pain ever since they were young children. If we contact the Scared Kid, Sarah may start to experience its pain directly, but the Scared Kid won't be exposed to any more pain than it is already feeling. I am explaining this to the Attacker.*

S: *(laughter)* We haven't done a very good job there—it's already feeling the pain.

J: I know it did its best, but it couldn't really protect the Scared Kid entirely, so it is carrying those memories and that pain. We're not going to make the Scared Kid feel worse. We're just going to witness the feelings it's holding and find out where it is stuck in the past.

My goal here was to get the Attacker to give us permission to work with the Scared Kid. However, to my surprise, this took the Attacker in a different direction—feeling bad that it hadn't succeeded in protecting the Scared Kid.

S: It's really, really sad that it failed because it tried so hard to protect the Scared Kid.

J: That is really sad. Let the Attacker know that if it gives you permission, we could actually heal the Scared Kid now, so it won't have to carry around this pain anymore.

S: It says, "It's hard to believe that you could do it when I couldn't do it. It's my job. I've got to be able to do it."

J: We're not going to try to protect the Scared Kid. We're going to heal it.

S: It's skeptical that you can do that because it's tried for so long.

J: I totally understand that. But you see, we have this really powerful method called IFS to help. That's why it's possible.

S: The Attacker doesn't like giving up. It has to be the one to do it. "It's got to be me. I've got to do it. I've got to be responsible for her."

J: Wow, this part really took on a heavy burden, being responsible for the Scared Kid.

It is now very clear that all the Attacker's attacks were really an attempt to protector this hurt exile. And it felt that **it** *had to do this because there was no help or support from anyone.*

S: Oh, yeah. There was nobody else to help so it never learned how to let anyone else help. I guess it feels ashamed that you could do it, when it couldn't. The Attacker is saying, "Then that reconfirms how useless and pathetic I am."

J: Well, tell the Attacker that it basically took on an impossible job. No child could have done that.

S: "Yes, that right. Not against them; they're too strong. There are too many of them, and I'm just a kid, you know."

Notice how all the Attacker's statements are in the present tense. It is really stuck in the past and experiences that time as if it were happening right now.

J: That's exactly right.

S: "I now realize that I'm just this little kid, and I'm trying to protect this other kid."

J: That's right; that's why it was an impossible job.

S: It's been trying to be an adult for so long. To protect itself from the adults, it had to take on an adult assignment. It had to grow really quickly. It didn't get to be a kid.

The Attacker Is Actually a Child

I was so moved! When I heard this sentiment during the session with Sarah, I had tears in my eyes. The Attacker was actually a child part that was intent on trying to protect the Scared Kid from pain. This is so different from the way we usually think of our Critics. It was also moving for Sarah and made it easy for her to feel compassion and caring for the Attacker. She saw that the real Attacker had been revealed, like the little man behind the curtain in the Wizard of Oz. And Sarah's image of the Attacker morphed again. Now she saw it as a frightened girl who was doing her best to act tough to prevent a terrible tragedy.

You may have noticed that there is a Criticized Child who is being hurt by the Attacker's attacks, and there is also an exile that the Attacker is trying to protect. In Sarah's case, these two are the same, the Scared Kid. The Attacker is actually hurting the very exile it is trying to protect. This is not unusual for Critics.

We can now expand our graphic to reflect this new understanding of the relationship between the Inner Critic and the Criticized Child.

Inner Critic Cluster

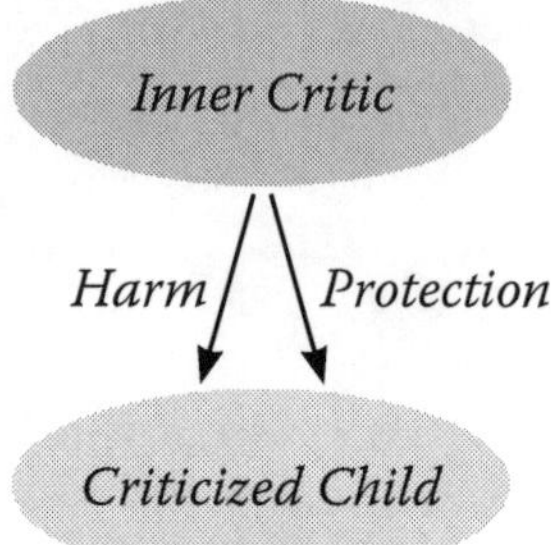

In Sarah's case, it looks this way:

Inner Critic Cluster

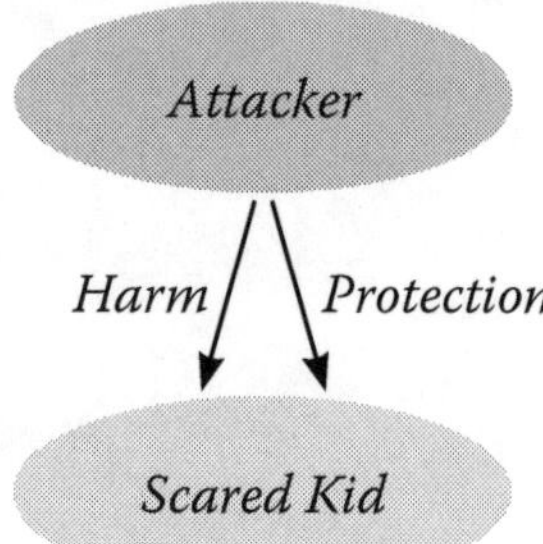

Your Critic's Positive Intent

Now that we know that your Critic is trying to help and protect you, let's explore further. Different types of Critics have difference motivations. Here are the main ones.

Protecting You from Judgment or Rejection

For some Critics, the primary goal is to protect you from being judged, ridiculed, rejected, attacked, or abandoned by people.

A Perfectionist Critic might be afraid that if you aren't perfect, you will be judged or dismissed, so it tries to get you to be perfect in everything you produce—even the way you look and operate in the world. It attacks you whenever you aren't top notch in every

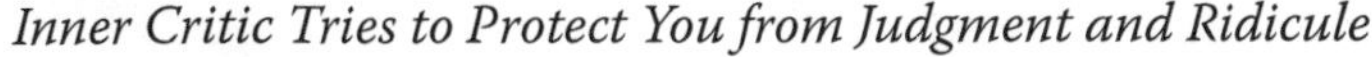

Inner Critic Tries to Protect You from Judgment and Ridicule

way. A Taskmaster Critic might try to get you to work hard so you will be really successful because it believes that if you fail at anything are or even just mediocre, you will be attacked or rejected. It is a slave driver that judges you unmercifully whenever you aren't working to maximum effort.

A Molder Critic might be afraid you are stepping outside the mold of what is acceptable, for example, by gaining weight, being angry, being needy or vulnerable, or being strong and visible. It might also be afraid of your being sexual, feminine, artistic, introverted, or emotional. The definition of what isn't acceptable varies from one Critic to another, but they all believe that if you violate these standards, you will be ridiculed and excluded by your family, friends, or a group that is important to you. So they attack and shame you whenever you do anything that strays from the mold.

Getting Approval

Some Critics are primarily trying to get approval, attention, or admiration from people who are important to you. Perfectionists and Taskmasters believe that if you are perfect or very successful, you will gain the attention you have always wanted. Molders believe that if you fit the mold of just who you parents or culture expect you to be—outgoing, intellectual, caring, beautiful, dutiful, or whatever was most valued—then you will finally get the love you so desperately need. They may want you to get approval from your boss or your boyfriend, but it really goes back to getting it from your parents or childhood friends.

They push you to be a certain way, and they may even reward you when you succeed. And of course, they attack you when you don't succeed.

Jay writes: I resolved most of my Inner Critic issues years ago. But when I *was* struggling with my Critic, it judged me for being shy and introverted, which I was. Its judgments were accurate but not very helpful. When I would hang back at a party and avoid reaching out to women I was interested in, my Critic would tell me I was a loser who would never find love. If a woman rejected me, it attacked me even more strongly by telling me there was something

Inner Critic Tries to Get Approval for You

wrong with me that made me unappealing to women. It was actually trying to motivate me to change—to become more outgoing, funny, confident, and so on—so I would attract women and find love. Of course, its judgments had the opposite effect. They made me feel bad about myself and less likely to take social risks.

Preventing Damage

Some Critics try to stop you from doing things that are harmful to yourself or others. An Inner Controller Critic might want to keep you from overeating or abusing drugs, or perhaps to stop you from flying into a rage or acting impulsively. A Guilt Tripper Critic might want to stop you from doing anything that causes another person pain, such as forgetting someone's birthday or inadvertently saying something hurtful. If you do something like this, it attacks and shames you to try to keep you from doing it again.

Keeping You Safe from Attack

An Underminer Critic may be afraid that if you are powerful or confident, you might put yourself out in the world. You might take risks such as writing an article, asking a woman for a date, or speaking up at work. This Critic is afraid that taking these actions will put you in harm's way. So it criticizes you to keep you scared and small so you will be safe. It wants to make you submissive so you won't assert yourself and put yourself in danger. When someone attacks you, a Destroyer Critic might blame you for it in an attempt to get you to change yourself rather than standing up to the person and triggering more attacks. For example, if your supervisor at work dismisses your ideas, your Critic will say it was your fault rather than seeing that he was overloaded with work and not paying attention. This self-blame also allows you to stay attached to the person, so you won't be alone. Even though the focus may be on current life relationships, the Critic's motivation ultimately goes back to keeping you safe from and connected to your parents.

Keeping You From Being Like a Parent

If you had a parent who didn't take care of you very well, or seriously harmed you, your Critic may feel extremely judgmental of that parent. It will also judge you harshly if you appear to be at all like that parent. For example, suppose you had a parent who was forgetful and disorganized, which resulted in your being neglected and abandoned. Your Critic may push you to be super responsible and attack you if you lapse at all because the Critic is reminded of your parent. Or if you had a parent who flew into rages and hit you, your Critic might judge you for feeling any anger or annoyance at all. The same may also happen if you were very embarrassed by one of your parents. For example, suppose your father was a drunken slob at times and embarrassed you in front of your friends. You might have a Critic that will attack you for drinking any alcohol at all or that will require you to be extremely neat in your appearance.

Exercise: Your Inner Critic's Positive Intent

Choose an Inner Critic part to focus on. Review what it says to you and which situations tend to trigger it.

What type of Inner Critic is it most like? Look over the seven types of Critics from Chapter 2, and guess or sense which one.

____

What is the Critic's positive motivation for you? Look over the various motivations we have just discussed and see if you can sense what this Critic is trying to do for you.

____

____

____

____

Example

Here is how Sarah filled out the sheet for this exercise:

What type of Inner Critic is it most like? Look over the seven types of Critics from Chapter 2, and guess or sense which one.

Destroyer
____

What is the Critic's positive motivation for you? Look over the various motivations we have just discussed and see if you can sense what this Critic is trying to do for you.

Attack me before my family does so the attack doesn't hurt so much.

Get a sense of power and not being crushed by being able to attack.

Creating a Profiles of Your Inner Critics

Throughout the rest of the book, we will be suggesting various exercises to help you get to know your Inner Critic parts. You can get assistance in doing this by using an application on our website (See Appendix B). The application allows you to create a profile of each one of your Critics, including what it says to you, what it looks like, the typical situations that tend to activate it, and its motivations. This application also allows you to profile your Inner Champion (see Chapter 11). We recommend that you begin using this program now and continue with it throughout the book whenever it seems as if it would be helpful.

Summary

In this chapter, you learned that your Inner Critic isn't as intimidating as it may seem and that it is actually trying to help you and protect you. We looked at the various positive motivations that different Critics may have, and you explored what motivates yours. Next you will learn how to separate yourself from your Critic and be open to getting to know it.

Chapter 5

Being Open to Your Critic

Healing takes courage, and we all have courage, even if we have to dig a little to find it.

—*Tori Amos*

It *is* possible to get to know our Inner Critics and connect with them. This strategy is far more effective than fighting with them and allow us to negotiate with them to relax so they will stop judging and pushing us so much. However, in order to do this, we must be both separate from the Critic and openly curious about it. This chapter shows you how to get to that place in yourself.[1]

Accessing Your Inner Critic

In an IFS session, we don't just understand our parts intellectually—we go inside and connect with them *experientially*.[2] We dialogue with them and develop a relationship with them. Therefore, in order to work with a part, you must access it experientially. You

1. It gives the specifics of how to use the material covered in Chapters 4, 5, and 6 in *Self-Therapy* when doing Inner Critic work.

2. This is step P1 in the IFS process; it corresponds to Chapter 4 in *Self-Therapy.*

can access a part through your body, your emotions, an image of what it looks like, or hearing its words. Most people access Inner Critic parts through hearing their attacking words and through images. For example, you might hear the Critic say that you are stupid, and you might have an image of it as a military sergeant.

You can also access parts through your body and emotions. However, if you try to access an Inner Critic part that way, you are likely to feel hurt, depressed, or hopeless, and you will sense how this feels in your body—perhaps a collapsed chest, a weight on your shoulders, or pain in your heart. These sensations are coming from the Criticized Child, not the Critic. It is useful to access those feelings and sensations, but remember to work with the two parts separately. Many people mix them up at first, which can be confusing and make your work difficult. Occasionally, someone does access the Critic through feelings or sensations. For example, you might feel tightness in your neck and jaw and a feeling of contempt. That would be the somatic (bodily) experience of the Critic.

The Self

In order to take the next step in the process, you must understand the *Self,* one of the most important concepts in IFS. We will describe it briefly here.[3] IFS recognizes that underneath all of our parts, every human being has a true Self that is wise, deep, strong, and loving. This is who we truly are when we aren't being hijacked by these painful or defensive voices. The Self is the key to healing and integrating our disparate parts through its compassion, curiosity, and connectedness. It is also the natural leader of our inner family, a guide through the adventures of life. IFS can help you access your Self, and from that place of groundedness and love, you can connect with your troubled parts and heal them.

Let's look at three qualities of the Self that are particularly important for psychological healing. When you are in Self, you will naturally embody these qualities.

---

3. For more detail, see Chapters 1 and 2 of *Self-Therapy.*

1. The Self is *connected.* When you are in Self, you naturally feel close to other people and want to relate in harmonious, supportive ways. You are drawn to make contact with them, to be in community. The Self also wants to be connected to your parts. When you are in Self, you are interested in having a relationship with each of your parts, including your Inner Critic, which helps them to trust you, opening the way for healing.

2. The Self is *curious.* When you are in Self, you are curious about other people in an open, accepting way. When you inquire into what makes them tick, it's because you want to understand them, not judge them. The Self is also curious about the inner workings of your mind. You want to understand why each part acts as it does, what its positive intent is for you, and what it is trying to protect you from. This curiosity comes from an accepting place, not a critical one. When parts sense this genuine interest, they know they are entering a welcoming environment, and they aren't afraid to reveal themselves to you.

3. The Self is *compassionate.* Compassion is a form of kindness and love that arises when people are in pain. You genuinely care about how they feel and want to support them through difficult times. When you are in Self, you naturally feel compassion for others as well as yourself. Your extreme parts are reacting to pain; some feel it, and some try to avoid

it. So compassion is really needed to hold, support, and nurture you while you take on very difficult material. When you are in Self, you feel compassion for your parts, and they can sense this, which makes them feel safe and cared for, so they want to open up and share themselves with you.

Blending

Blending is a key concept in IFS that we describe here with respect to Inner Critic work.[4] At any given moment, you are either in Self, or a part is blended with you. You are either feeling calm, curious, open, and compassionate because you are in Self, or you have been taken over by a part and are engulfed in its feelings and beliefs. This understanding is signified by the concept of the *Seat of Consciousness.* Whoever resides in the Seat of Consciousness at any given moment is in charge of your psyche at that point. The Self is the natural occupant of the Seat of Consciousness. However, if a part blends with you, it takes over the Seat and determines how you feel and react.

Let's look at how this concept applies to Inner Critic work. When you are judging yourself, an Inner Critic part is blended with you. When you are feeling bad about yourself, a Criticized Child part is blended with you. In fact, often both the Critic and the Criticized Child are blended with you at the same time, which means that they both occupy the Seat of Consciousness, and the Self is pushed into the background.

You can only work successfully with an Inner Critic if it isn't blended with you. Imagine a situation in which a father repeatedly punishes a child in a harsh way. What can be done about this? The child can't do anything. She is too young and scared. She has no power or perspective. The father can't do anything because he believes he is right. He is caught up in his judgmental role. Only a third person could intervene and change things. In your internal world, *you* can become that third person when you aren't being either the "father" (the Critic) or the child. That means you must unblend from them.

---

4. For more detail, see Chapters 5 and 6 of *Self-Therapy.*

Critic and Child Blended with Self

Self is pushed behind the Seat of Consciousness into the background because the Critic and Child have taken over the Seat.

When you unblend in this way, it doesn't mean that the self-judgment disappears or you stop feeling bad about yourself. It just means that you aren't completely taken over by these feelings. You have some space inside that is separate from them. Your Self has regained the Seat of Consciousness, and the Critic and Child have moved aside. You don't fully buy into the idea that you are inadequate. You can see that this idea is just the result of a part attacking you rather than believing it is the truth about you. For example, when your Critic says that you are a loser and will never find love in your life, you recognize that this is simply an attack from this part of you. It isn't the truth.

Self Unblended from Critic and Child

Self resides in Seat of Consciousness. Critic and Child have stepped aside.

Though you may still feel sad or ashamed, when you are unblended from the Critic and Criticized Child you aren't dominated by these feelings. You have a place in you (Self) that is feeling solid and calm. From this place, you can view these feelings, understand these attacks, and work with them. Parts of you may feel hurt to hear this message that you are a loser and hopeless about your love life, but that isn't all that's going on. You reside in a place that is deeper than those emotions, a place of calmness and curiosity.

Unblending from Your Critic and Criticized Child

This section of the chapter shows you how to unblend from these parts and reside in Self during an IFS session.[5] This is not the final solution to your Inner Critic problem. It is just a preliminary step that gives you enough space to deal with the problem.

5. This is step P2 in the IFS process; it corresponds to Chapter 5 in *Self-Therapy.*

Remind yourself that feeling worthless is just the result of an Inner Critic attack and not the truth about you. This will go a long way toward helping you to unblend from the Critic and Child. If this reminder isn't enough, there is more you can do.

If you are scared of the Critic or feel crushed by it, or if you feel depressed, sad, hopeless, or worthless, remember that these feelings come from your Criticized Child, not from your Self.

Take a few moments to access the nurturing side of you (which is an aspect of Self) so you can take care of your Criticized Child. Now focus on those sad, hopeless feelings, which gives you access to the Criticized Child. Let it know that you understand its hurt and feel compassion for it. Give the Child some time to take in your caring. Then you can ask the Child if it would be willing to step aside into a safe place and let you get to know the Critic from the place of Self. Explain that the Self is powerful and will be connecting with the Critic but it won't allow the Critic to attack.

You can also step back from the Child into Self or see an image of the Child at a distance from yourself. Another option is to take a moment for a short centering meditation to help you access Self. (See *Self-Therapy* for details.)

If more is needed, evoke an image of a powerful, caring part that can be with the Child to keep it safe from the Critic.

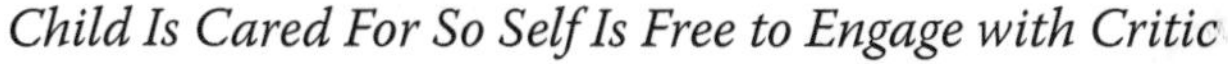

Child Is Cared For So Self Is Free to Engage with Critic

Or visualize the Critic contained in a room, so it is less threatening, while you look at it through a window. This is usually enough to help the Child to feel safer and separate from you. If it still isn't able to, you may need to spend some concentrated time with the Criticized Child. Let go of trying to work with the Critic for now, and take the time to get to know the Child and develop a relationship with it in which it really feels safe and connected with you. This will make it much easier for the Child to unblend.[6]

Let's look at an example of unblending from Sarah's session with her Inner Critic, which she called the Attacker. Her Criticized Child is the Scared Kid.

Sarah's Inner Critic Cluster

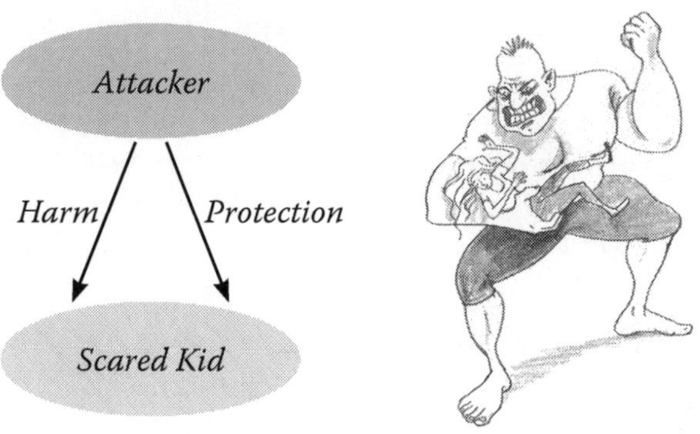

We will look at a segment of the session that came before the one in Chapter 4. Here Sarah has just accessed the Attacker.

Jay: Check to see how you're feeling toward the Attacker right now.

Sarah: Well, I'm really scared of it.

J: OK, that probably means that you're blended with the Scared Kid. So ask the Kid if it would be willing to step aside into a

---

6. If you are still unable to get the Criticized Child to unblend, then you probably need more help with this work than you can get from this book. You might consider taking one of our Inner Critic or IFS classes or working with an IFS therapist. See Appendix B for these resources.

safe place. And let it know that we're going to work with the Attacker to understand it and connect with it. And we're not going to let it do more attacking. We're going to try to connect with it. See if the Scared Kid would be willing to step aside for you to do that.

S: Yeah, so now it has stepped aside.

Once you are separate from the Criticized Child, you can continue on to the next step.

The Value of Being Open to the Critic

By now you have learned that your Inner Critic part is trying to help you and protect you from pain. This means that you don't have to fight it or argue with it. You don't have to try to overcome it or get rid of it. You can connect with it and develop a cooperative, trusting relationship. This is the best way to help the Critic to relax and ultimately to transform.

In order to do this, you must be in Self with respect to your Inner Critic. You need to be openly curious about it and respectful of it. It can tell if you feel negatively toward it, and it probably won't show you much about itself other than attacking you. Let's consider our earlier metaphor with the harsh father (Critic) and the hurt child. In order for change to occur, a third person (Self) must intervene. But this person can only make a difference if the father trusts her. If he feels that she is judging him for the way he is treating his child, he won't give her the time of day. She must genuinely be interested in where he is coming from; then he might listen to her.

Unblending from Your Inner Defender

This section of the chapter shows you how to unblend from a part that prevents you from having the open curiosity and compassion of Self.[7] To check to see if you are in Self, notice how you feel

7. This is step P3 in the IFS process; it corresponds to Chapter 6 in *Self-Therapy*.

toward your Inner Critic right now. Do you like it or hate it? Do you appreciate it or judge it? Do you want to banish it? Are you afraid of it? Are you curious about it? The purpose of this inquiry is to discover whether you are in Self with respect to the Critic. A key principle in IFS is that all parts are welcome. This means we need to be genuinely open to getting to know each part from a curious and compassionate place will encourage it to reveal itself.

This stance is not always easy to come by, especially with a Critic. If it has been causing you pain, it would be natural for you to be angry with it. It would be understandable that you might judge it and want to be rid of it. However, approaching the Critic (or any part) with these attitudes won't lead to healing and reconciliation. It isn't likely to trust you or open up. In fact, this attitude isn't coming from your Self—it is coming from another part of you, which we call the *Inner Defender*[8] because it wants to defend you from the Critic. Often the Inner Defender feels judgmental and angry toward the Critic; it may try to dismiss the Critic or even banish it from your psyche. However, you can't get rid of a part, and the Critic usually just fights back against attempts to dismiss it.

Inner Defender

Sometimes your Inner Defender tries to argue with the Inner Critic. If the Critic says that you are worthless, the Defender tries to prove that you are a good person who has accomplished things in your life. If the Critic says you can't succeed, the Defender argues that you can. If the Critic says you are a lazy bum who must work harder, the Defender may say, "Leave me alone." It wants to engage with

8. The Inner Defender is one kind of concerned part, as described in *Self-Therapy,* Chapter 6.

the Critic and defend your goodness and your right to be yourself. It wants to fight against being controlled by the Critic. For example, Sarah wanted to convince her Critic that she was a valuable person who could make it in the world. This is a worthwhile assertion of your value; it makes sense that your Inner Defender wants to champion you. However, engaging with the Critic in this way usually doesn't work. The Critic often wins the argument. Or if your Inner Defender wins for now, the Critic may redouble its attacks later. And this approach creates inner conflict.

Once you realize that you are blended with the Inner Defender, ask that part if it would be willing to step aside so that you can get to know the Critic from an open place. Explain that doing this will help you to work successfully with the Critic to help it relax and transform. You might first need to give the Defender some space to express its judgments and concerns about the Critic. If the Defender has expressed itself and still isn't willing to step aside, ask what it is afraid would happen if it did. Then reassure it about its fears. You may need to explain that you won't let the Critic take over and start attacking you again.

For example, at first Sarah was angry at her Critic, the Attacker, and wanted to get rid of it because it caused her so much fear and pain. Clearly she wasn't in Self. She needed to get her Inner Defender, which she called the Blamer, to step aside so she could be open to the Attacker. Let's see how that happened:

Sarah: Now that the scared part has stepped aside, the Blamer comes out.

Jay: That part is blaming the Attacker?

S: Yeah, we don't like it, we don't like being criticized all the time … so a bit of a feeling of resentment toward the Critic comes out.

J: So ask the Blamer if it would be willing to step aside in order for you to work with the Attacker in a way that will help the Attacker to be less critical and to let go of its role.

S: It's amazing how strong that part is. It wants to get in there and fight the Attacker.

Inner Defender Blended with Self

Blamer has taken over the Seat of Consciousness

J: So maybe it needs to be heard a little more. Does the Blamer need to speak about its feelings toward the Attacker?

S: Yes. Coincidentally, just last week, I actually stood up to my mom for the first time ever. I really told her I was fed up with her criticizing my life. I'd never let the Blamer really tell her before, so it's in its power at the moment and wants to stay there.

J: That makes a lot of sense. It sounds as if it was a really good thing that the Blamer stood up to your mother.

S: Yeah, it really likes to tell her off, and tell the Attacker off. So how do I get it to step aside?

J: Well, you might explain to the Blamer that the Attacker is different from your mother. It may be modeled after your mother, but the Attacker is actually a part of you. It's actually trying to help you, in its own distorted way.

S: OK. It can begin to see that.

J: And see if the Blamer might be willing to step aside and let you connect with the Attacker and help it to let go.

S: Yup. That works.

J: So it's willing to step aside? Thank the Blamer for that. That's a big thing to do.

S: It was the way you put it. It made it easier.

Self Unblended from Inner Defender

Blamer has stepped aside.
Self resides in Seat of Consciousness and can get to know Critic.

In IFS, you don't try to get to know your Critic (or any part) unless you are in Self, which means that you feel open to it and want to understand it from its own point of view. Once Sarah was able to unblend from the Blamer, she could be open to her Inner Critic from Self. This is the best place from which to be successful in working with the Critic.

If your Inner Defender isn't willing to step aside, focus your attention on it for a while and get to know that part. Once it trusts you, it will probably step aside.[9]

When you are in Self, you are interested in knowing what makes the Critic tick, how it sees the world, and what it is *trying* to do for you. You can sympathize with the Critic's need to avoid pain and protect you from harm. This doesn't mean that you allow the Critic to keep attacking you. It doesn't mean that you believe its judgments of you. You stay in Self, where you are separate from the Critic and can see that it is causing you problems, but you are nevertheless open to getting to know it because you know its heart is in the right place. You are interested in connecting with it in order to ultimately transform it.

Even though we are using categories of parts, such as Inner Critic, Criticized Child, Inner Defender, and so on, remember that each of your parts is unique. Please call your parts by whatever names seem right. Don't feel as though you must use Criticized Child or Inner Defender. Each of your parts will have its own unique characteristics. For example, your Criticized Child won't be the same as anyone else's, and you might have more than one Criticized Child part, each of which is different. Don't try to put your parts in boxes according to our descriptions of these categories. Discover your own parts and their unique attributes.

---

9. If you try all these suggestions and the Defender still won't step aside, you may need additional support with your Inner Critic work, such as an Inner Critic class or IFS therapy.

The Inner Critic Cluster

This graphic shows the Self and the various parts that we have discussed so far in the Inner Critic cluster. Notice that the Inner Defender is polarized with the Critic. This means they are at war with each other. The Self is able to cooperate with all the parts, even though they may be fighting each other. The Inner Critic is harming the Criticized Child as well as trying to protect it, and the Inner Defender is trying to protect the Child.

Inner Critic Cluster

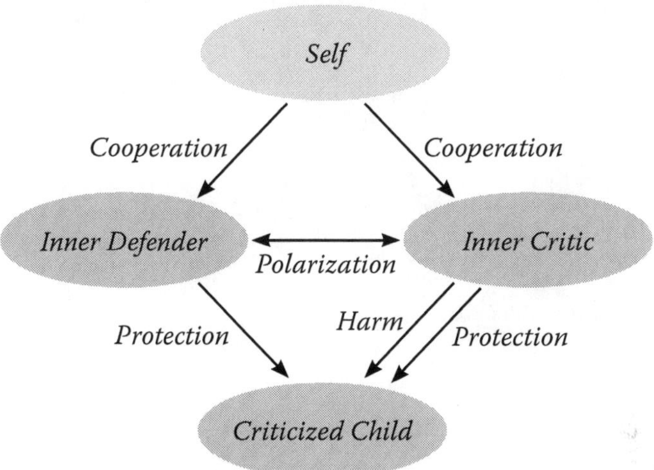

Polarization, an important concept in IFS, refers to a situation in which two parts are in conflict with each other. They are fighting with each other over what you should feel or how you should act. For example, the Inner Defender and the Inner Critic are fighting over whether or not you (the Criticized Child) should feel bad about yourself or OK.

We can now view Sarah's version of this graphic, showing her parts.

Sarah's Inner Critic Cluster

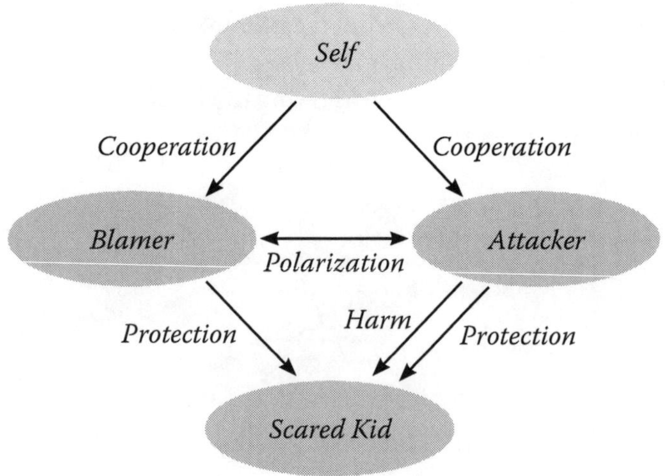

Exercise: Unblending

This exercise takes you through the steps as described in this chapter. Choose one situation in which one of your Inner Critics usually attacks you. Imagine that this situation is happening right now. What is your Inner Critic saying to you?

____

____

____

____

Close your eyes and allow an image of the Inner Critic to emerge. Or access your Critic through your body or feelings.

If you are scared of this Inner Critic or feel crushed by it, those feelings are coming from the Criticized Child. Take notes about these feelings.

Check to see if you have an image of the Criticized Child.

Ask the Criticized Child to step aside into a safe place (maybe with a strong protector) or visualize the Critic in another room (as described above).

Remember that this Inner Critic is trying to help you and protect you. See if you can be open to learning about it from its perspective.

If you are angry at the Inner Critic or want to argue with it or get rid of it, that is completely understandable, but it won't help in getting to know the Critic. These feelings indicate that you are blended with your Inner Defender.

Ask that part what its concerns are.

Validate its concerns, and then ask the Defender to step aside so you can be successful in working with the Critic.

If it steps aside, check again to see how you are feeling toward the Critic.

___

If there is another Inner Defender part, ask it to step aside, until you are finally in Self with respect to the Critic. (This means that you are openly curious about the Critic and interested in learning about it from its perspective.) How do you feel toward the Critic now that you are in Self?

___

___

Ask the Critic to tell you or show you what it is trying to accomplish by judging you.

___

___

___

Example

Here is an example of how Sarah filled out this sheet when she did the exercise:

Choose one situation in which one of your Inner Critics usually attacks you. Imagine that this situation is happening right now. What is your Inner Critic saying to you?

You're less than nothing.

You don't deserve to even be here. Get lost!

Close your eyes and allow an image of the Inner Critic to emerge. Or access your Critic through your body or feelings.

A huge powerful monster with great muscles and a loud voice that is attacking me.

If you are scared of this Inner Critic or feel crushed by it, then those feelings are coming from the Criticized Child. Take notes about these feelings.

Scared of it.

Check to see if you have an image of the Criticized Child.

Battered and crushed.

If you are angry at the Inner Critic or want to argue with it or get rid of it, that is completely understandable, but it won't help in getting to know the Critic. These feelings indicate that you are blended with your Inner Defender.

Blamer.

Ask that part what its concerns are.

Doesn't like being criticized. Wants to get rid of the Attacker. If it stepped aside, the Attacker would really take over and make me miserable.

Validate its concerns, and then ask the Defender to step aside so you can be successful in working with the Critic.

How do you feel toward the Critic now that you are in Self?

Open and interested in what it is about.

Ask the Critic to tell you or show you what it is trying to accomplish by judging you.

Attack me before my family does so it doesn't hurt so much.

Get a sense of power and not being crushed by being able to attack.

Summary

In this chapter, you learned how to access your Inner Critic and how to unblend from it and from your Criticized Child. You also learned how to check to see if you are open to getting to know the Critic and to unblend from your Inner Defender. Now you are ready to get to know your Critic and discover its positive intent.

Chapter 6

Befriending Your Inner Critic

> The journey to discovery with my clients has led to astounding conclusions about who we really are. Not only are we much more at our core than we could imagine, the very aspects of us that we thought proved our worthlessness are actually diamonds in the rough. We are inherently good through and through.
>
> —*Richard C. Schwartz,*
> *Introduction to the*
> *Internal Family Systems Model*

Now that you are in Self, the next step in your IFS session is to get to know your Inner Critic and develop a cooperative relationship with it. This will provide the basis for further healing and transformation.

Discovering Your Critic's Positive Intent

The first thing you want to do is discover your Critic's positive intent—its motivation for attacking you.[1] In this section, we show

1. This is step P4 in the IFS process, covered in Chapter 7 of *Self-Therapy*.

how to apply this step to Inner Critic work. We know that your Inner Critic thinks attacking you will help you, so you can ask it some questions to find out its rationale. A good question to start with is, "What are you trying to accomplish by judging (or shaming or pushing, etc.) me?" Make sure you are asking this question from genuine curiosity—not, "How could you possibly think this will help me, you stupid jerk?" Find the place inside you that is truly interested in finding out what this part is trying to do for you. Ask from that place.

Follow up this first question with any others that naturally come up for you as you hear the Critic's answer. For example, if it says it is trying to get you to work harder, you might ask how it thinks judging you will make you work harder. Or you might ask what it hopes you will get by working harder. If you aren't sure why this part started judging you just now, you might ask what just happened that made it decide that it was important to judge you.

Eventually, it is important to ask, "What are you afraid would happen if you didn't tell me I'm ugly?" (Or whatever it says to you.) The Critic's response often provides a deeper understanding of what it is trying to protect you from. Recall in Chapter 4 how Sarah's Critic was trying to protect the Criticized Child from the attacks of her family.

Dealing with a Mistrustful Critic

Sometimes a Critic won't easily answer these kinds of questions. Some Critics will keep attacking you instead of answering. Some Critics will say that they aren't trying to accomplish anything. "You are just a loser (or worthless, etc.), and I just want you to know that." Some may refuse to talk to you at all. In all of these cases, the Critic doesn't really trust you.[2]

When a Critic acts in these ways, it usually means that it doesn't really believe that you want to get to know it. It believes that you just want to get rid of it. This belief isn't all that surprising because

2. Dealing with mistrustful protectors is covered in Chapter 8 of *Self-Therapy.*

there are probably parts of you that *do* want to get rid of it. In fact, it is often the case that those parts have recently been quite active. Maybe you just got one of those parts to step aside in order to get into Self. It's no wonder the Critic isn't ready to trust you so fast.

Let's return to the metaphor of the harsh father, the child, and the third person. It's as if the third person (you) has been judging the father and telling him that he is treating his child badly. His response has been, "Get lost. She's my kid, and I'll treat her the way I want." Now you have suddenly switched to being genuinely interested, without judgment, in why he is treating her this way. It's not surprising that he might be taken aback and not trust you yet.

If a Critic resists your questions in any of these ways, ask, "What are you afraid would happen if you did dialogue with me and answer my questions?" It will usually say, "You will try to stop me from doing my job," or "You will try to get rid of me." Reassure it that you aren't trying to do either of these things. The way IFS works is that we never try to force a part to change or give up its job. And we never try to get rid of a part. Of course, we are hoping that your Critic will relax and choose a new role in your internal system, but only if it wants to—never through coercion. We just want to get to know it, discover its motivation, and connect with it. Any further change will happen as the work develops, but only if the Critic chooses this because it no longer feels a need to protect the exile in the same way.[3]

Transcript: Working with a Mistrustful Critic

Here's how the work described above happened for George, one of Jay's clients. We've included a transcript of part of a session with his Critic. George has already accessed the Critic and unblended

3. If your Inner Critic still won't answer your questions, you might need more help with this work than you can get from this book. You could take an Inner Critic class or work with an IFS therapist. See Appendix B for these resources.

from his Criticized Child and Inner Defender, so he is now in Self and ready to get to know the Critic.

Jay: Ask the Critic to tell you what it's trying to accomplish by judging you the way it does.

George: It's not letting me know. It just wants to start berating me again.

George's Slave Driver Critic

J: So ask it if it doesn't trust you or if it doesn't trust me.

G: It doesn't care.

J: So it just wants to berate you; it doesn't want to talk about what its role is. Is that right?

G: Yeah.

J: So ask it what it's afraid would happen if it answered that question and talked about its role. If it were willing to talk to you about the judgments, what is it afraid would happen?

G: That you'd make it go away.

Slave Driver Fears Being Banished

J: OK, I can understand why it might think that. So explain to the Critic that we're not going to try to make it go away—that we never try to make any parts go away, we don't coerce them, and we're not trying to fight with them. We're actually interested in getting to know the Critic and making a connection with it.

G: It says, "I enjoy doing this job."

Here it is still not answering the question, but I ask in a different way in hopes that it will.

J: OK. So ask it what it's trying to accomplish by doing the job.

G: It says it is trying to get me to work hard and do well. I'm so lazy! I need to try harder.

Slave Driver Opens Up to George

It looks as if the Critic has accepted what I said and is trusting us enough to go on because it is now beginning to answer the question about its motivation. Now we can proceed to get to know it.

Transcript: Discovering Your Critic's Motivation

We will now continue with George's transcript to see how he found out what his Critic was trying to do for him.

J: OK. The Critic is trying to motivate you to try to work more, is that right?

G: Yes. It wants me to be smart and please my boss, not let things go until the last minute and then do a poor job. I am going to call it the Slave Driver.

J: Ask it what it hopes you will get by working harder and pleasing your boss.

G: It wants him to like me and appreciate me. It wants me to get better assignments and get put on more interesting jobs and teams. It wants me to get a raise.

J: It wants you to get approval and the benefits that accompany that.

G: Yeah. The real issue is that the Slave Driver wants my boss to think I'm really competent and smart.

J: And what does it hope that you will get from that?

G: I will get in with my boss … and I'll feel really good about myself. That's what it wants.

J: OK. That makes sense. I appreciate that goal. Ask the Slave Driver how it thinks that judging you will get you this. How will judging you get you to work harder?

G: Well, it figures that if it pushes me to work hard and judges me when I don't, then I will eventually get the message. I will buckle down and do good work.

J: Uh huh. I see that.

G: Although it is doubtful about my ability to really change. It says I'm hopeless.

Slave Driver's Goal

J: Ask the Slave Driver what it is afraid would happen if it didn't push you and judge you.

G: It says, "Hah! It would be like now, only worse. You would just be lazy and avoid doing the work. You would really be a failure, and your boss would really look down on you—even worse than he does now. At least now, I get you to do some work. I keep you from being a complete deadbeat."

Slave Driver's Concern

J: So the Slave Driver wants to protect you from being looked down on by your boss. And, of course, it really wants you to get his approval.

G: Yes, that's right. The Slave Driver says that you understand it.

J: Does that make sense to you, what the Slave Driver is trying to do for you?

G: Yes. I see it.

George now understands the Slave Driver's positive intent, and the Slave Driver sees that he does, so we can now move on to solidifying George's relationship with the Slave Driver.

When you have discovered the positive intent of one of your Critics, you might want to update your profile for that Critic on our website (see Appendix C).

Developing a Trusting Relationship with Your Critic

Discovering the Critic's positive motivation isn't enough. It is also important to develop a relationship in which it trusts that you appreciate its efforts and roughly share its goals. Most of the time, the Critic has a faulty and damaging strategy for reaching its goals, but the goals themselves are often quite valid. For example, George's Critic wants him to be appreciated by his boss, to be successful, and to feel good about himself. There's nothing wrong with that.

When you genuinely connect with the Critic and it trusts you, it is much more likely to relax its need to judge you. It may actually listen when you tell it that the judgments are causing serious problems for the Criticized Child. The Critic is likely to be interested in better strategies for achieving its goals that don't harm your self-esteem. Recall our metaphor of the harsh parent and child. If you, as the third party, can show the parent that you sympathize with his situation and appreciate his efforts to parent his child well (even though he is actually harming the child), then he is likely to listen to you when you tell him that he needs to find a more helpful way of doing it.

In many cases, the Critic has been a pariah in the internal system, hated by other parts because of the pain it causes. It often feels isolated and (ironically) judged by other parts. Or it may be involved in constant conflict with another part. So when you connect with the Critic, it often feels touched and relieved that its positive intent is finally recognized. And this helps to relieve some of the constant internal conflict you may have been suffering from.

Once you understand what your Critic has been trying to do for you, see if you appreciate it for trying to protect you and help you. Even if you don't like the pain that the Critic has been causing, perhaps you can see that its heart is in the right place. If so, communicate that appreciation directly to the Critic. Once you have done this, check to see how the Critic is responding. You will find out whether you have reached the Critic, whether it is taking in your appreciation, or whether it still doesn't trust you. Proceed with whatever additional work needs to be done to solidify your relationship with the Critic.

Transcript: Developing a Relationship with Your Critic

Let's now continue with George's session to see how he connects with the Slave Driver.

Jay: Do you have some appreciation for the Slave Driver's efforts on your behalf?

George: Yes, I actually do now. I see that it has really been trying to help me in this weird way.

J: OK. So let the Slave Driver know about your appreciation of it.

G: *(laughs)* It says, "It's about time that somebody saw me. You've been beating me up and trying to get rid of me for so long." Actually, I told the Slave Driver that I'm sorry. I didn't realize that it was trying to help me.

J: And how is it responding to you?

G: It's softening now. It's feeling relieved to not have to fight all those other parts in order to do its job. It says, "Somebody had to do this job. Somebody had to get you going, and no one else was doing it, so I had to. And then you hated me. And all these other parts tried to beat me up."

J: So it has been getting flak for doing the job it felt had to be done.

G: Yeah.

J: How is it responding to your appreciation?

G: It says, "This feels a lot better."

Slave Driver and George Have a Trusting Relationship

Now that George and the Slave Driver are connected, this sets the stage for further steps in healing, which we will discuss in the next few chapters. We can show the beginnings of the cluster of George's parts.

Inner Critic Cluster

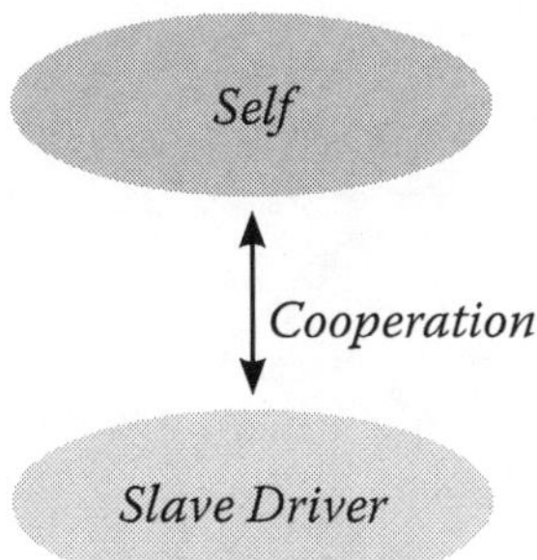

Exercise: Getting to Know Your Inner Critic

Choose an Inner Critic part to work with and do an IFS session in which you follow steps P1–P5. Use the Help Sheet below to guide you in this process. Afterward, write down what you have learned about the part.

What it is trying to accomplish by judging and pushing you

____

____

What it is afraid would happen if it didn't do this

____

____

What it is trying to protect you from

____

____

Its response to your understanding and appreciation of its efforts on your behalf

---

It might be useful to add this information to your profile for this Critic on our website.

Example

Here is what George filled out:

What it is trying to accomplish by judging and pushing you

Make me work hard and get my boss's approval.

What it is afraid would happen if it didn't do this

I would be lazy and a complete failure.

My boss would really think badly of me.

What it is trying to protect you from

Failure and shame.

Its response to your understanding and appreciation of its efforts on your behalf

Feels better, relieved, softening.

Help Sheet 1:
Getting to Know Your Inner Critic

You can refer to this Help Sheet to guide your steps while you are working on yourself.

It can also be used when you are facilitating for a partner.

1. Getting to Know the Inner Critic

P1. Accessing the Critic

If the Critic is not activated, imagine yourself in a situation in which it judges you.

Get an image of it and hear what it says to you.

P2. Unblending from the Criticized Child/Critic

Check to see if you are feeling bad about yourself or are believing that you are deficient.

Options for unblending:

- Remember that this is just a message from the Critic and not the truth.
- Listen to the Criticized Child's pain with compassion from Self.
- Ask the Criticized Child to go into a safe place so you can help both it and the Critic.
- Explain that you won't allow the Critic to attack it.
- Supply a nurturing aspect of Self to comfort the exile.
- Visualize the Critic in a room to provide a safe container for it.

P3. Unblending from the Inner Defender

Check to see how you feel toward the Critic right now.

If you feel compassionate, curious, etc., then you are in Self-leadership; move on to P4.

If you don't, then unblend from the Inner Defender as follows:

Ask if it would be willing to step aside (or relax) just for now so you can get to know the Critic part from an open place. Explain that doing this will help you to connect with the Critic and help it to change, and that you won't let the Critic take over and attack.

If the Defender is willing to step aside, check again to see how you feel toward the Critic, and repeat.

If it still won't step aside, ask what it is afraid would happen if it did, and reassure it about its fears.

P4. Finding Out about the Critic

Ask the Critic what it is trying to accomplish by judging you.
Ask what it is afraid would happen if it didn't.
Sense what exile it is trying to protect.

P5. Developing a Trusting Relationship with the Critic

You can foster trust by saying the following to the Critic (if true).

- I understand what you are trying to do.
- I appreciate your efforts on my behalf.

Summary

In this chapter, you have learned how to get to know your Inner Critic and discover what it is trying to do for you. You have also learned how to create a trusting relationship with your Critic. From this base, you can heal your Criticized Child or directly work on releasing your Critic from its judgmental role. In the next chapter, we will explore how criticism plays out in relationships.

Chapter 7

Criticism in Relationships

> You take your life in your own hands, and what happens?
> A terrible thing: no one to blame.
>
> —Erica Jong

So far, we have been exploring self-criticism by your Inner Critic and how to transform it. However, criticism is also a major factor in most relationships, and many interpersonal problems are related to the Inner Critic. This chapter looks at the situation in which your criticism is directed at someone else and how your parts react when someone criticizes you.

The Judge

Most of us are judgmental of other people at times, even if we don't necessarily express our judgments. In this book, we call the part that criticizes others the *Judge* to distinguish it from the Inner Critic. However, in some cases, your Inner Critic might be the part that turns its judgments on others, so there might not be two different parts.

People often become judgmental of others in order to protect the Criticized Child. Something happens that triggers the pain of the Criticized Child. Maybe you feel rejected by someone, or perhaps you don't do well on a test or project. This prompts your Criticized Child to feel inadequate or worthless, and it may also trigger your Inner Critic to attack the Child. The Judge is a protector of the Child, so it may jump in and criticize the person who rejected you or the person who gave you the test, or even the entire educational system. If the Judge can prove that the other person is at fault, your Criticized Child doesn't have to feel bad. This strategy is also an attempt to counter the Critic's judgments of you; if the other person is bad, then you aren't.

The Judge sometimes also comes forward to protect a different exile. Perhaps someone didn't give you the support you needed from him or her on a day when you were feeling sad. This brought up pain in one of your exiles, so you judged that person to keep from feeling this pain.

This doesn't mean that it is never valid to notice shortcomings in other people, but the Judge often criticizes them to ward off our own underlying shame or self-attacks. The Judge can be just as harsh and punitive as the Inner Critic, and it can be just as painful for someone else to receive judgment from you as it is for you to receive it from your Inner Critic. In fact, this dynamic is a major factor in most relationship difficulties. Often both people are judging each other, triggering the pain of their exiles, and then protecting with more judgment, causing a vicious cycle of hurt feelings, arguments, and resentment.

We can add the Judge to the cluster of parts related to the Inner Critic. It is polarized with the Critic and protecting the Child.

Inner Critic Cluster

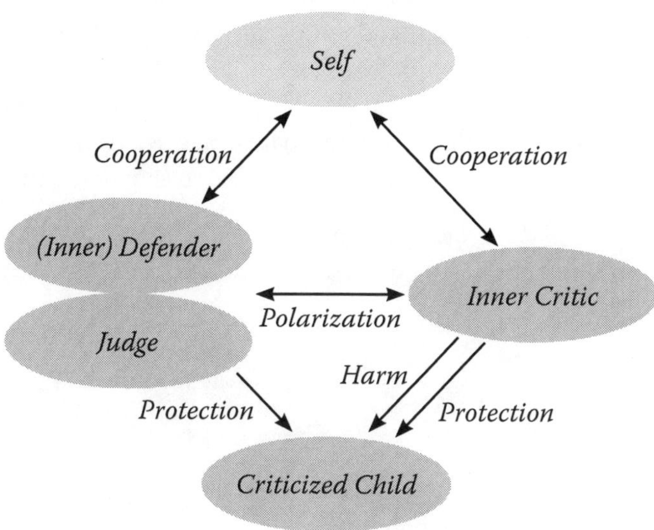

Reacting to an Outer Critic

We will now discuss what happens when *another person* criticizes you. This tends to trigger most of the parts in the cluster.

The Criticized Child gets activated because it believes the criticism and feels bad about itself.

The Inner Critic may become activated because it feels validated and thinks its job is to criticize you more. It may say, "See, I told you that you were no good. This proves it." Of course, the Critic often becomes triggered in an attempt to protect the Criticized Child from outer criticisms. It doesn't see that it is just making the Child feel worse.

The Defender often gets triggered in an attempt to protect the Child. It argues with the person who judged you in order to prove them wrong and exonerate the Child. The part that we called the Inner Defender is now an Outer Defender as well, so we'll just call it the *Defender*.

The Judge may get in on the act, supporting the Defender in protecting the Child. It says, "Not only is the judging person wrong, but it is actually their fault, not yours." This, of course, will often trigger the other person's Criticized Child and then their Defender and Judge, making them criticize you more. You can see how this could easily lead to a knockdown, drag-out fight. However, the more you have healed your Criticized Child and transformed your Critic, the less likely you are to get caught in such a situation.

Let's look at an example of the parts that get triggered by an outer criticism. In the illustration below, Bill's wife berates him for

Parts' Reactions to External Criticism

watching TV and not fixing the sink. This triggers his Critic to tell him that he has failed to live up to how he should function as a husband. In Bill's internal system, it is his Criticized Child who feels the impact of this judgment. A Judge part tries to put the blame on Bill's wife in order to protect the Child.

Remember not to force your parts into these categories; get to know each part as a unique entity. For example, you might have three different parts that would be considered a Criticized Child. Each will be different from the others. Or you might have one part that is both a Defender and a Judge.

It is worth remembering that you may have these reactions to someone, even if they aren't judging you. All it takes is that your parts *perceive* them as judging you. Or they may be mildly judging, and your parts may perceive them as being very harsh. This is often how a fight starts. Minor acts of judgment lead to reactions, which trigger greater judgments, and around and around you go.

Exercise: The Parts Triggered by an Outer Critic

Think of a person who judges you and upsets your parts.

____

Imagine that you are in a situation in which that person is criticizing you.

____

____

____

Hear what the person is saying.

Notice how this makes you feel. You will probably be having more than one reaction. Focus on one of your reactions, access the part that is having that reaction, and get to know it briefly. Then answer whichever of the following questions are appropriate. Not all of them will be relevant for each part. And you may not have time to get to know the part well enough to answer all of them. Just do whatever you can.

Part

Which category does it fit from the cluster?

What does it feel?

What is it trying to accomplish internally?

What is it trying to accomplish externally?

____

____

Which part is it fighting with?

____

Which part is it protecting?

____

Then look for another feeling reaction, access that part, and get to know it, as above. Keep going until you have gotten to know each part that was triggered.[1] Once you have finished, check the Inner Critic cluster to see if you missed a part. This doesn't mean that all the parts in the cluster will necessarily be triggered. It is just a way to perhaps discover another part that is activated.

1. This kind of process is described in more detail in Chapter 4 of *Self-Therapy* under "Accessing Parts from Current Experience."

Example

Let's look at an example of how one of our clients did this exercise.

Think of a person who judges you and upsets your parts.

My wife
____

Imagine that you are in a situation in which that person is criticizing you.

When I have forgotten to do something I said I would do or something important to her.

Hear what the person is saying.

You never listen to me. You don't really care about me.

Notice any parts that are having a reaction.
Part 1

Little Joey

Which category does it fit from the cluster?

Criticized Child

What does it feel?

Inadequate, not good enough

Part 2

Shamer

Which category does it fit from the cluster?

Critic

What does it feel?

Judgmental, annoyed

What is it trying to accomplish internally?

Not sure

What is it trying to accomplish externally?

N/A

Which part is it fighting with?

Defender

Which part is it protecting?

Not sure

Part 3

Defender

Which category does it fit from the cluster?

Inner Defender

What does it feel?

Angry

What is it trying to accomplish internally?

Defend against attacks from the Shamer

What is it trying to accomplish externally?

Defend against the accusation from my wife

Which part is it fighting with?

Shamer

Which part is it protecting?

Little Joey

Summary

In this chapter, you learned about your Judge part, which can criticize other people. You also explored what happens with your parts when someone judges you. In the next chapter, we will look at various possibilities for how your Criticized Child was wounded when you were young.

Chapter 8

Origins of Your Criticized Child

Perhaps everything terrible is in its deepest being something helpless that wants help from us.

—Rainer Maria Rilke

Let's look at common childhood situations that lead to the wounding of child parts and the activation of Inner Critic parts. You will use this information in the next chapter when you learn to heal your Criticized Child.

Judgment

Children are often criticized or judged by parents, family members, or other important people in their lives. If this happened to you frequently or harshly, a child part that started out innocent and whole would end up feeling wrong, bad, inadequate, or worthless, depending on the kind of judgments you received. This is the part we call the Criticized Child. If the judgments were accompanied by anger, yelling, or physical abuse, the Child would be traumatized.

Judgment can take a variety of forms. Almost all parents have certain standards for your behavior, such as performing at a high level, not showing emotions, being proper, or taking care of others. If they only loved and approved of you when you met those standards and criticized you for any failure to meet them, this would have an impact on your Criticized Child. Perhaps a parent got frustrated with you because he had no tolerance for your process of learning, so he ended up judging you instead of helping you with homework. Maybe a parent didn't recognize when you couldn't clean your room well because you were too young, and she flew off the handle at you.

Your father may have used criticism as a means of motivating you. He thought that judging you and comparing you to others would encourage you to work hard and succeed. Perhaps he focused only on your shortcomings and never praised you for your strengths or successes. Any of these actions, if done repeatedly, would wound your Criticized Child and leave it with feelings of low self-esteem and incompetence.

Modeling vs. Internalization

In most cases, parental criticisms will also cause an Inner Critic part to start judging us in ways that are similar to the way our parent did. Let's discuss why this happens. The conventional psychological explanation uses the concept of *introjection* or *internalization*. It says that you internalize what your parent did, which means that your Inner Critic is simply a copy of your parent. If a parent criticized you in a certain way, your Critic will criticize you in a similar way. In this view, Critics don't have their own "personhood" and motivation. They simply mimic what your parent did. If this were true, the only solution would be to ignore your Critic, overpower it, or get rid of it.

However, IFS has discovered that Inner Critic parts aren't just mechanical copies of your parents. (This understanding is not unique to IFS. Voice Dialogue and other approaches that work with subpersonalities have come to the same conclusion.) Critic parts often model themselves after what your parent did when you were a child, but they have their own motivations in your current life. For example, if your father judged you as lazy, your Inner Critic might do the same thing, but not simply because it was copying your father. Most likely it would be judging you to get you to work hard so you wouldn't be judged by your father. Its *strategy* for protecting you is modeled after you father, but its *reason* for judging you is to protect you from your father.

You might say, "This doesn't make sense because the Critic is causing a lot of damage right now." And you'd be right. It is using a misguided attempt to protect you from something that happened decades ago when you were young. The Critic doesn't realize the damage it is causing, but the good news is that it *is* trying to help you. This means that you are actually on the same team. So you can connect with it and work with it, which you couldn't do if your Critic were only a mechanical internalization of your father.

Let's look at this situation through a metaphor. A couple hundred years ago, most doctors didn't understand germs or the need for hygiene; they bled people to heal them, with knives that weren't sterile and may even have been rusty. If you went to one of these doctors, he might actually make you sicker. However, since he would want to help, you could work with him to find a better strategy for healing you. The same applies to an Inner Critic—since it is trying to help, you can work with it.

In some cases, it is more complicated than this. Suppose your father judged you as lazy to try to get you to work harder. Then, when your Inner Critic is judging you as lazy to get you to work harder, it has modeled itself after both your father's motivation and his judgmental behavior. So this situation makes the Critic look even more as though it is simply a copy of your father. However, the central IFS view of parts still holds. The Critic is judging you because it thinks that doing so will help you, and therefore you can develop a cooperative relationship with it. That is the bottom line.

Shame

If you were shamed or ridiculed by parents, teachers, or your peers, this would cause your Criticized Child to carry shame or embarrassment. This experience could also prompt an Inner Critic to shame you in an attempt to keep you from doing whatever led

Child Taking on Mother's Shame

to your being shamed in the first place. Your Child might also carry shame if your parents or family felt ashamed about something such as poverty, or their race or religion, or if their community looked down on them. Children tend to take on the shame of their parents as their own, and it resides in the Criticized Child part.

Punitive Control

Children often do things that are dangerous to them, such as touching a hot stove or running into the street. Therefore, their parents need to stop them and teach them that these actions should be avoided. If your parents overreacted and were punitive in trying to stop you, they may have accomplished their objectives, but your Criticized Child would be harmed in the process. The same problem can happen when parents try to stop a child from hurting other children. If you hit other kids or took their toys for your own, as many children do, your parents needed to teach you not to do those things. However, if they did this in a harsh, demeaning way, it would make your Child feel bad about having those natural impulses. This harshness would then activate an Inner Critic that wants to protect you from your parents. However, the Critic (probably an Underminer or Guilt Tripper) is likely to use the very same harsh approach that your parents did. After all, they are the models it has for its behavior. So it will produce the very harm to your Criticized Child that it is trying to prevent.

Being Attacked or Not Wanted

If your parents didn't want you, or if one of them abused you physically, your Criticized Child would end up feeling that it didn't have the right to exist or that it was dangerous to exist. So a Destroyer Inner Critic may actually try to kill you or crush you so you aren't there in order to keep you safe, as strange as that sounds.

If a parent attacked you repeatedly, your Critic might blame you for the attacks, which would make your Criticized Child believe it was your fault. It does this so you won't fight back and be harmed

Parent's Rejection of Child is Origin of Destroyer

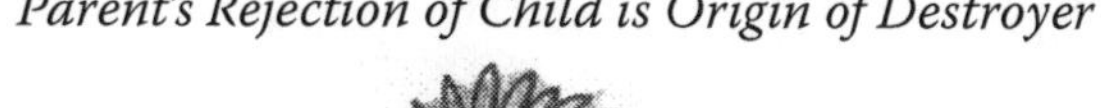

even more. Taking on the blame also allows you to stay connected to the attacker, which is often crucial when you depend on a parent. It would have been too scary to see how abusive they were. Your Critic turned its anger on you since it wasn't safe to get angry at them.

Another reason your Critic might attack you is to be in control of the attacks. This is preferable to being at the mercy of the unexpected attack from a parent. Your Critic would then feel as if it had some power in an impossible situation. Its attacks would also shut you down so you wouldn't be vulnerable when an attack came from your parent.

This feeling of being at fault can happen even without any blame or attack from outside. If something bad happened to you as a child, such as getting very sick or a parent being depressed, your Criticized Child may assume it was your fault, even if there is no reason for this, and even if you weren't blamed by your parents. This assumption gives the Child the illusion of being able to change the situation. "If I did it, then maybe I can fix myself and stop it."

Let's look at another example. Suppose that there was a mismatch between your energy and your mother's; she was outgoing and you were introverted, or vice versa. It would be natural for you, as the child, to feel that there was something wrong with you because you weren't like her, even if she didn't judge you for the difference. After all, she is the model you have for how a person is supposed to be. You might even try to be like her, but that would be impossible because your natural inclination is different. Your Criticized Child is likely to believe that there is something wrong with you for being different from her.

Guilt

Parents often use guilt to control children. Your parents may have told you that you were a bad person when you wanted special attention or demanded a particular Christmas present, which is perfectly normal behavior for a child.

Perhaps they made you feel guilty by acting like martyrs and giving you responsibility for taking care of their pain and making them feel good. They may have blamed you for their problems

Origin of Guilt

and feelings, or even just turned to you for support too often. This would make your Criticized Child feel guilty, and it might activate a Guilt Tripper Critic that tried to stop you from doing the "bad" things or force you to try to take care of your parents.

When Being Strong or Visible Wasn't Safe

If you were judged or ridiculed whenever you were strong, visible, or capable, this would wound your Criticized Child and also a trigger a Critic that tried to undermine you to keep you small, hidden, and safe. Your parents might have said, "Who do you think you are?!" Perhaps you were rejected or abandoned for being powerful or standing out, or for being better than a sibling or your parents in some way. Or maybe your parents felt bad about themselves when you outshined them, and you felt responsible for their feelings. This could trigger an Underminer Critic that tries to prevent you from being noticed in order to protect you.

Summary

Keep in mind that these childhood situations can vary from mild to very intense. Some Criticized Child parts experienced judgments that weren't too harsh or only happened occasionally, and so they ended up with mild pain and feelings of inadequacy. Other Child parts were seriously wounded and carry intense pain, crippling feelings of worthlessness, or perhaps even trauma. The intensity of an Inner Critic's attacks will often be proportional to the degree of wounding of the Criticized Child.

In this chapter, we have explored some of the typical childhood relationships and situations that can wound your Criticized Child. In the next chapter, you will learn how to heal this Child using IFS.

Chapter 9

Healing Your Criticized Child

> There came a time when the risk to remain tight in a bud was more painful than the risk it took to blossom.
>
> —Anias Nin

Your Inner Critic is trying to protect your Criticized Child or to protect you from the pain the Child carries. So a good way to help your Critic to let go of its judgmental role is to heal the Child first. Then the Critic doesn't need to protect it so much. In this chapter, we will show how to adapt the IFS process of healing an exile to work with the Criticized Child.[1]

There are two reasons to heal your Criticized Child. (1) It allows your Critic to let go of its judgments. (2) The wounds that the Child carries are affecting your feelings and behavior, even when your Critic isn't attacking. These wounds make you feel insecure, scared, worthless, ashamed, depressed, and so on. Therefore, healing your Criticized Child will help you feel better about yourself even before your Inner Critic changes.

---

1. This involves steps 2 through 7 in the IFS process, covered in chapters 10–14 in *Self-Therapy*.

Getting Permission to Work with Your Criticized Child

Before you work with an exile, you must get permission from any protectors that think this isn't safe; otherwise, they will sabotage the process. Since your Inner Critic is protecting your Criticized Child, you start by asking the Critic's permission to make contact with the Child. It usually gives permission fairly easily, but it is still important to ask. It also is a good idea to check to see if there are any other protectors that don't want you to access the Criticized Child, and then ask their permission as well. If a protector is reluctant to give permission, this is because it is afraid of what would happen if you worked with the Child. Ask it about this fear, and then reassure it.[2] If it is afraid that you will be flooded by the pain of the Child, you may first need to negotiate with the Child to not overwhelm you (see Unblending from the Criticized Child below) before the Critic will give its permission.[3]

Getting to Know Your Criticized Child

Accessing the Criticized Child

The next step is to get to know your Criticized Child.[4] First you access the Child by feeling its emotions, sensing it in your body, or getting an image of it, just the way you would with any part.[5] You might have an image of the Child as a wounded waif in a burned-out

---

2. This is Step 2 of the IFS process, as described in Chapter 10 of *Self-Therapy*. Step 1 is getting to know a protector, in this case the Inner Critic, which we have already covered.

3. If you are still unable to get permission to work with your Criticized Child, you probably need more help with this work than you can get from this book. You could take one of our Inner Critic or IFS Classes, or you might prefer to work with an IFS therapist. See Appendix B for these resources.

4. This is Step 3 in the IFS process, as described in Chapters 11 and 12 of *Self-Therapy*.

5. Step E1, Chapter 12 in *Self-Therapy*.

building. You might feel its pain as a knife in your chest or as a dark, empty hole in your gut. You might feel its hopelessness as a gray fog that seems never ending.

Unblending from the Criticized Child (Again)

Accessing the Criticized Child can bring up considerable pain. So, if necessary, unblend from the Child so you aren't flooded by its pain. This allows you to be available to comfort and help it. You may have already done this unblending earlier in the IFS procedure, but now that you are explicitly accessing the Criticized Child, its emotions may be more intense, so you may need to repeat the process. This is especially important when you are working with a Criticized Child part who was seriously wounded. You unblend in a way that is similar to what was described in Chapter 5 of this book. You ask the Child to separate from you so you can be there to help it. Make it clear to the child that if it separates, you won't ignore it; you actually want to get to know it and heal it. You can also step back from the Criticized Child so you have a place to stand where you aren't overwhelmed by its emotions.[6]

Unblending from the Critic (Again)

Now check to see how you are feeling toward the Criticized Child. If you are feeling curious and compassionate toward it, you are in Self and can get to know it. However, you might realize that you are feeling judgmental toward the Child, which means that you are blended with the Critic. Even though you unblended from your Inner Critic earlier in the process, now that you are about to connect with the Criticized Child in a direct way, the Critic's judgments of the Child may be triggered, and it may blend with you again. You must unblend from the Critic or from any other

6. Unblending from an exile is Step E2 in the IFS process, covered in Chapter 11 of *Self-Therapy*.

concerned part so that you are fully in Self with respect to the Criticized Child;[7] only then can you heal it.

Critic parts often feel that the Criticized Child is a "bad" part that has gotten you into trouble and caused pain in your life, so they naturally want to get rid of it. They don't want you to get to know it because that would bring up its shame and make you feel more inadequate or worthless. Critics don't really understand that *they* are causing the Child to feel this way.

Explain to the Critic that if it lets you work with the Child, you can heal its pain and depression so it won't ruin your life anymore. Ask the Critic to step aside and let you get to know the Criticized Child and transform it. Once the Critic understands what you are aiming for, it will usually agree to this.[8]

Getting to Know the Criticized Child and Connecting With It

The next step is to get to know the Child. You find out what pain it feels in response to the Critic's attacks and what negative beliefs it has about itself.[9] The Child often feels worthless, depressed, hopeless, hurt, or ashamed. It may believe that it is inadequate, bad, stupid, crazy, ugly, or repulsive. These feelings and beliefs are the direct result of the Critic's attacks on you. The Criticized Child is the part of you that is being harmed by these attacks.

You also need to develop a relationship with the Child.[10] You will probably feel caring and compassion for it as you hear what it is feeling. Let it know how you feel toward it and check to see how it is responding. Make sure it trusts you and is taking in your caring

---

7. Step E3, Chapter 12 in *Self-Therapy.*

8. After following these suggestions, if you are still unable to get the Criticized Child or a concerned part to unblend, you probably need more support with this work than you can get from this book. If you run into trouble at a later point in your work with the Child, you might also need more help. You could take one of our Inner Critic classes or go into IFS therapy.

9. Step E4, Chapter 12 in *Self-Therapy.*

10. Step E5, Chapter 12 in *Self-Therapy.*

before going on. If you don't feel caring toward the Child, it means that you aren't in Self. Check to see what concerned part has taken over and work with it to step aside, as discussed above.

Accessing and Witnessing the Origins of Your Criticized Child

The feelings and beliefs that the Child carries have two different causes. One is the Inner Critic's attacks in your current life, and the other is what happened in childhood—often criticisms from parents, teachers, or other children. Though the Critic is indeed causing you pain, it is really adding to the pain that your Criticized Child already carries, which originated when you were young. The Critic is triggering this childhood pain and making it worse. In IFS, an important step in the healing process involves uncovering the situations that caused that pain in the first place.

Ask the Child to show you a memory or an image of what happened when it was young to cause it to feel so bad about itself. It will show you situations like those we discussed in the previous chapter. Witness these early memories, relationships, and situations from Self—with caring and compassion for the pain of the Criticized Child.[11]

Witness what the Child shows you about what happened and how that made it feel emotionally. It is usually not necessary for you to fully re-experience these feelings, just to witness them. However, this must be from a place of empathy, not a removed or purely intellectual place. That wouldn't be Self. Continue witnessing until the Child has showed you everything about this situation that it wants to. Then check to see if the Child feels that you understand how bad it was, and if necessary, have it show you more until it feels that you get it. Then you can move on to reparenting.

---

11. This is Step 4 of the IFS process, described in Chapter 13 of *Self-Therapy.*

Reparenting Your Criticized Child

Now you (in Self) enter the scene of the childhood wounding in your imagination to help the Criticized Child. You relate to the Child in whatever way it needed someone back then. You give it what it needs to heal what happened or to change its experience. This can be a variety of things, depending on which of the situations discussed in Chapter 8 actually occurred.[12] Here we look at how to reparent a Criticized Child part who was judged, shamed, or attacked.

There are two types of reparenting that the Criticized Child is likely to need. (1) You protect the Child from the criticism and attack by stopping the parent (or other person) from doing it. This can be done in a number of ways. You can do it by imaging yourself standing between the parent and the Child in that original scene. You will be able to stop the parent because in Self, you can be bigger and more powerful than any image of a parent, if necessary. You can assert your strength and authority and tell the parent that you won't allow him to criticize and attack anymore. You can explain to the parent that this is not helpful and show him how this behavior is actually harming the Child. Most parents don't really want to hurt their children, so the parent figure may offer to change its behavior as a result of your intervention. You can also support the Criticized Child in standing up to the parent if she wants to.[13]

(2) The other type of reparenting that is often needed is validation. Because you are in Self, you have the ability to give the Child anything she needs. Accept her just the way she is. Give her your love and caring. Express your appreciation of who she is. This will help the Child begin to feel good and valuable rather than bad and worthless.

Just telling the Child that she is OK or good isn't personal enough. The message needs to come from you in a contactful way. You might say that you love her and value her just the way she is. If your Child received conditional approval from her parents, tell

---

12. This is Step 5 in the IFS process. The details of how to reparent an exile are discussed in Chapter 13 of *Self-Therapy*.

13. Chapter 13 of *Self-Therapy* contains a transcript that shows how this kind of reparenting works.

her that you value her just for being herself, and she doesn't have to do anything at all to get your appreciation. This is crucial. The main message that your Criticized Child needs to hear is that she is lovable and valuable, that she is precious. However, she won't get it just because you say she is (though that helps). She will get it when she experiences that *you* love her and value her, that she is precious to *you*. This is a personal statement from you, not an abstract statement about her worth.

You will naturally feel this way toward her when you are in Self. If you aren't feeling this way, check to see if a concerned part is in the way, and work with it to get it to step aside.

Self Gives Child Love

If your Criticized Child was blamed for something that she didn't do, tell her in no uncertain terms that what happened wasn't her fault. If your Child was criticized for not doing something that she shouldn't have been asked to do, such as taking care of an inept parent, let her know that it wasn't her responsibility. If she was attacked for something that *was* her fault, help her see that she didn't deserve such nasty treatment in response. Maybe she did need to learn to behave differently, but she isn't bad and she didn't deserve to be attacked and shamed for her behavior. If the Child wants you to, you can even tell the parents that they shouldn't have treated her that way.

Even though it isn't possible to change what happened in the past, it is possible to change the way those experiences are held and structured in your psyche. That is what reparenting does, along with retrieval and unburdening, the steps that come next. And that is what is needed to transform your life in the present.[14]

Retrieving Your Inner Child

Sometimes the Child will want to be taken out of that harmful childhood situation and brought into a safe place.[15] You want to bring her into a place where she will be safe from attack and shame and where she can be with you to receive your caring and appreciation. This can be a place in your current life, such as your backyard. It can be a place in your body, perhaps next to your heart. Or it can be any imaginary place where she would enjoy being, such as at a beautiful beach. The Child should be in charge of the retrieval, choosing whether or not she wants to be retrieved and where she would like to go.

---

14. See Chapter 13 of *Self-Therapy* for a fuller discussion of this.

15. This is retrieval, Step 6 of the IFS process, described in Chapter 13 of *Self-Therapy*.

Unburdening Your Criticized Child

A burden is a painful emotion or negative belief that an exile takes on as a result of what happened in childhood. A Criticized Child is likely to have taken on emotions such as shame, guilt, hurt, or depression. She might have taken on the belief that she is bad, inadequate, incompetent, worthless, unimportant, weak, mediocre, lazy, stupid, or ugly. If the Child was also attacked or harshly shamed, she may also have taken on the burden of feeling frightened and unsafe. It is useful for the Child to release these burdens in an unburdening ritual done in the imagination. She finds where these burdens are lodged in her body and then releases them to one of the natural elements (light, water, wind, earth, or fire) so they can be carried away and transformed.

After the burdens are released, the natural positive qualities and feelings of the Child will spontaneously arise. She is likely to feel valuable, lovable, and OK just as she is. She may also feel certain positive things about herself that were blocked by the judgments from childhood. She might feel good, strong, beautiful, competent, intelligent, hardworking, and so on. You can aid the process of integrating these qualities by paying attention to what arises and spending time embodying them and enjoying them.

Transcript: Healing George's Criticized Child

Let's now continue with George's session from Chapter 6. His Inner Critic is called the Slave Driver.

Inner Critic Cluster

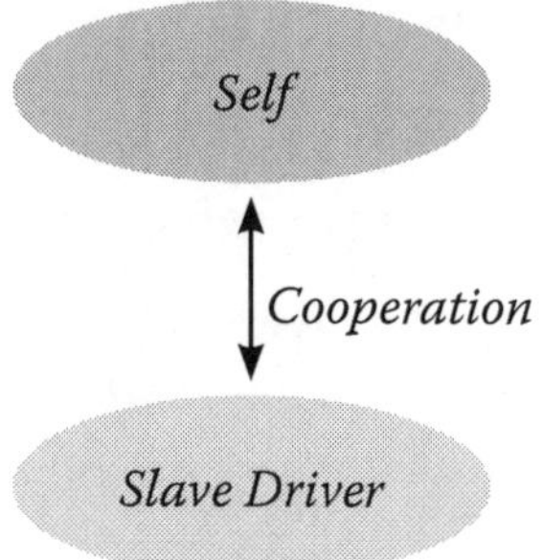

We pick up the session after George has gotten to know the Slave Driver's positive intent and made a connection with it.

Jay: It seems that the Slave Driver is trying to protect you from being a failure and getting disapproval from your boss. Is that right?

George: Yes.

J: So I imagine that the Slave Driver is trying to protect a part of you that has been judged as a failure. Ask it if that's right.

First we need to identify the exile that the Slave Driver is protecting—the Criticized Child.

G: Yes, it says it is doing that.

J: So, ask it if it will give you permission to get to know that part it is protecting.

G: It says, "Sure. Go ahead. I'm tired of doing this. Maybe you can do better."

J: OK. Thank it for that.

We get permission to work with the Child.

Now focus on the part that has been judged. Let me know when you have a sense of it.

G: *(pause)* OK. I can feel it in my belly. It feels empty and like a dull ache.

J: Can you see an image of what that part looks like?

G: *(pause)* Yeah. It looks like a Little Boy doubled over and holding his stomach. He looks really down.

George accesses his Criticized Child, the Little Boy.

J: Check to see how you are feeling toward him.

This question checks for two things: (1) If George were blended with the Little Boy, he wouldn't be able to answer the question because he would be *the Little Boy. Since he can answer it, he probably isn't blended with the Boy. (2) It checks to see if George is in Self with respect to the Boy.*

G: Well, mostly I feel interested in him. But there is a part of me that looks down on him. I don't want to have anything to do with him. He is such a loser, and he gets in my way so often these days, when I feel like I can't do things well.

J: So there is a part of you that is judging and dismissing him.

G: Yeah, I guess so.

George isn't in Self. He is blended with a concerned part, which might even be the Critic, so now I will help him unblend.

J: OK. Explain to that part that if it lets us work with the Little Boy, we can heal him of his bad feelings about himself so he won't get in your way anymore.

G: That sounds hopeful.

J: See if that part would be willing to step aside so you can be open to the Little Boy, because that will allow us to do this healing work.

G: Yeah. It's willing.

J: Great. Check to see how you are feeling toward the Little Boy now.

G: I'm really interested in getting to know him.

Here is the graphic showing more of George's cluster of parts. We have added an arrow between Self and the Criticized Child showing the healing relationship.

George's Inner Critic Cluster

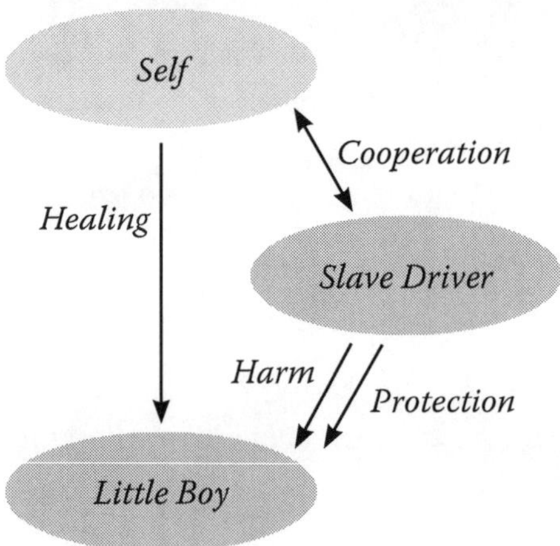

Now George is in Self, so we can move on to getting to know the Criticized Child.

J: OK. Ask him to tell you or show you what he is feeling.

G: He feels really bad about himself. He says he is a loser; he can't really do things well. He just thinks he can't pull it off, being successful. He's inadequate.

J: He believes he can't do things well.

G: Yeah. He'll never get seen and appreciated at work. (pause) He feels really sad about that. I can feel the sadness in my chest and eyes.

Now that we understand something about how the Little Boy feels, I want to discover the origins of these feelings in George's childhood.

J: Ask him to show you a memory or an image of what happened when he was little to make him feel this way.

G: I have a sense of my father being frustrated with him. Oh, he's trying to do homework, and my father is supposed to be helping him with it. But he's angry at the Boy.

J: How old is the Boy?

G: It seems like he's 7 or 8. (pause) My father is totally frustrated with the Little Boy. He's yelling and screaming at him. He says the boy is stupid and lazy. "What's the matter with you, you lamebrain!"

J: Wow. Ask the Boy how that makes him feel.

G: Like a piece of crap. And scared, too. (pause) He feels really low, like there is something seriously wrong with him. Totally worthless.

J: And how are you feeling toward the Little Boy as you hear about this?

G: I feel a lot of compassion for him.

Witnessing

Self is witnessing Little Boy's memory of his Dad being angry with him.

J: Let him know that. Communicate your compassion to him in some way.

I have George communicate his compassion to build his relationship with the Little Boy. This is important for healing in IFS.

G: He likes that. (pause) Now he feels angry, too. He's mad at his father for doing that. The Boy says, "It's not fair. I was doing my best. It was hard homework. And he didn't even give me a chance to learn it. He just flipped out."

J: Yeah. Let the Boy know that you welcome his anger. You are here to witness whatever he feels.

Anger is a valid feeling for an exile. It needs to be witnessed as much as more vulnerable feelings do.

Criticized Child Expressing Anger

G: OK. He is yelling at his father.

(pause) Now the Boy is calming down.

J: See if there's more that he wants you to know about what happened or how it made him feel.

G: He felt all alone. There was no support for him anywhere. He just had to take this crap.

J: Yes, I understand that. *(pause)* Ask the Little Boy if that is everything, or if there is more that he wants you to know.

G: He felt ashamed of himself, like he wasn't worthy. A deep sense of wrongness. Like he was born flawed. This kind of thing, his father going bananas, happened many times.

J: Wow. That sounds awful. *(pause)* Ask him if he feels that you understand how bad this was for him.

Before you can move on to healing the Criticized Child, it is important that it feels that Self really understands its pain.

G: He says I get most of it, but he doesn't think I really understand how terrible he felt.

J: Ask him to show you whatever he needs to, so you really get that.

G: OK. Now I am feeling more of the Little Boy's shame and feelings of worthlessness.

J: Is it OK for you to be feeling that much of his pain, or is it too much?

Here I am checking to make sure that George isn't too blended with the Little Boy, because then the healing wouldn't be successful, and George might be retraumatized.

G: No, it's fine. I actually feel relieved to fully experience it.

Since George says he is OK with the pain, I know he is still in Self, even though he is feeling some of the Little Boy's emotions. This is called conscious blending.

J: Ask him if he now believes that you get how bad it was.

Conscious Blending

George is in Self even though he is feeling the Little Boy's pain.

G: Yes, he does. He is happy to have someone understand how horrible it was. He feels lighter now.

Now the witnessing is complete, so we can move on to reparenting.

J: Good. Now I would like you to enter that scene with the Little Boy and your father, and be with the Boy in the way he needed someone to be with him then. Give him whatever he needs to feel better or to change what happened.

G: *(pause)* Well, he wants me to hold him. *(pause)*

J: Go ahead and do that.

G: OK. And I'm telling him that he didn't deserve to be treated that way. That he was a good student; he just had some trouble with homework sometimes, and his father couldn't handle that.

J: *(pause)* See if there is more that he needs from you.

G: Yes. I'm telling him how much I appreciate the things he's really good at. Music and spelling and writing and sports—that he was smart and competent. *(pause)* But more important, I just appreciate him for being himself. I have a real sense of that now. I feel like I'm really in contact with him, and I just love him and value him. It's hard to explain.

J: You don't need to. Just communicate that to him directly from your heart. That's more important than the words.

G: Yes. He's taking that in.

J: Good. *(pause)* See if there's anything else the Little Boy needs from you.

G: No. He's feeling good. He's beginning to feel like he is OK as he is. *(pause)* He feels more at ease.

J: What does that feel like in his body?

G: He feels relaxed in his shoulders, and a kind of bright feeling in his heart, like open and full.

Now the reparenting is complete. It doesn't seem like retrieval is needed, so I move on to the unburdening step.

J: Great. Now ask him if he would like to release those burdens, those painful feelings and negative beliefs that he took on as a result of the way your father treated him.

G: Yes, he would love to do that.

J: OK. What are those feelings and beliefs?

G: Well, mainly feeling worthless and inadequate, and sad about that.

J: And where has he been carrying those burdens in his body or on his body?

The Little Boy's Burden

G: In his heart, as a black weight, like a stone.

J: OK. We will help him to release it. He can give it up to light, or have it washed away by water, or blown away by wind, or put it into the earth, or burn it up in fire, or anything else that feels right.

G: He wants to bury that stone in the earth.

J: OK. Set up that situation for him.

G: We are going into a wilderness. *(pause)* I'm helping him take the stone out of his heart, and we're digging a hole on the side of a mountain.

J: Good. Take as much time as he needs. Feel that stone leaving his body as you do this.

G: The stone is in the ground, and it's raining a lot, and the water is helping to dissolve the stone into the earth. And all the yuckiness is draining away and being renewed by the earth.

J: *(pause)* Let me know when it's all gone.

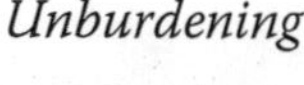

Unburdening

G: *(pause)* Yes, now it is.

J: Now notice what positive qualities or feelings are arising in the Boy now that this burden is gone.

Now that the burden is gone, the Boy can experience his natural, healthy state.

G: It's similar to what happened a couple of minutes ago—a warm, good feeling in his heart. Like he is valuable, like he is precious, even.

J: Wonderful. Take a few minutes to really enjoy that, to bask in it.

G: *(pause, sigh)* It feels so good.

George has now healed his Little Boy, his Criticized Child. As you can see, this is beautiful work, and very valuable in itself. And it also sets the stage for transforming the Critic.

Transformed Child

Exercise: Healing Your Criticized Child

Do a session in which you heal a Criticized Child. Proceed through all the steps described in this chapter. Use the Help Sheet below to guide you. Then fill in the answers below that are relevant to your work.

Criticized Child

____

If the Child was blended with you, how you unblended

____

____

____

If there were concerned parts, their fears and how you reassured them

Child's feelings and beliefs

What situations caused it to feel that way

What happened in childhood

How that made the Child feel

What form of reparenting you gave the Child

Burdens the Child carried

____

Where it carried the burdens in its body

____

What element the burdens were released to

____

Positive qualities that emerged

____

Example

Here is how George filled out the sheet:

Criticized Child

A Little Boy doubled over and holding his stomach.

If the Child was blended with you, how you unblended

N/A

If there were concerned parts, their fears and how you reassured them

Part says he gets in my way by making me feel like I can't do things.

I explained that we can heal him so he won't make me feel that way anymore.

Child's feelings and beliefs

Feels really bad about himself, sad. He's a loser, inadequate.

He'll never get appreciated at work.

What situations caused it to feel that way

Work

What happened in childhood

Father yelled at him and called him lazy and stupid.

How that made the Child feel

Scared, worthless, all alone with no support.

Angry at father

What form of reparenting you gave the Child

Held him. Told him he didn't deserve that treatment.

Gave him appreciation and love.

Burdens the Child carried

Worthlessness, inadequacy, sadness.

Where it carried the burdens in its body

A black stone in his heart.

What element the burdens were released to

Earth, water.

Positive qualities that emerged

Warmth in heart, value, preciousness.

Help Sheet 2: Healing Your Criticized Child

You can refer to this Help Sheet while you are working on yourself to guide your steps.

It can also be used when you are facilitating a partner.

2. Getting Permission to Work With Your Criticized Child

If necessary, ask the Critic to show you your Criticized Child.

Ask its permission to get to know the Child.

If it won't give permission, ask what it is afraid would happen if you accessed the Child.

Possibilities are:

- The Child carries too much pain. Explain that you will stay in Self and get to know the Child, not dive into its pain.
- There isn't any point in going into the pain. Explain that there is a point—you can heal the Child.
- The Critic will have no role and will therefore be eliminated. Explain that the Critic can choose a new role in your psyche.

3. Getting to Know Your Criticized Child

E1: Accessing the Criticized Child

Sense its emotions, feel it in your body, or get an image of it.

E2: Unblending From Your Criticized Child

If you are blended with the Child:

- Ask the Child to contain its feelings so you can be there for it.

- Consciously separate from the Child and return to Self.
- Get an image of the Child at a distance from you.
- Do a centering/grounding meditation.
- If the Child won't contain its feelings:
- Ask it what it is afraid would happen if it did.
- Explain that you really want to witness its feelings and story, but you need to be separate to do that.
- Conscious blending: If you can tolerate it, allow yourself to feel some of the Child's pain.

E3: Unblending Concerned Parts

Check to see how you feel toward the Child.

If you aren't in Self or don't feel compassion, unblend from any concerned parts. They are usually afraid of your becoming overwhelmed by the Child's pain or the Child taking over.

Explain that you will stay in Self and not let the Child take over.

E4: Finding Out about Your Criticized Child

Ask: What do you feel? What makes you feel so bad about yourself?

E5: Developing a Trusting Relationship with Your Criticized Child

Let the Child know that you want to hear its story.

Communicate to it that you feel compassion and caring toward it.

Check to see if the Child can sense you, and notice if it is taking in your compassion.

4. Accessing and Witnessing Childhood Origins

Ask the Child to show you an image or a memory of when it learned to feel this way in childhood.

Ask the Child how this made it feel.

Check to make sure the Child has shown you everything it wants you to witness.

After witnessing, check to see if the Child believes that you understand how bad it was.

5. Reparenting Your Criticized Child

Bring yourself (as Self) into the childhood situation and ask the Child what it needs from you to heal it or to change what happened.

Protect it from being attacked or shamed.

Communicate to it your love, acceptance, and appreciation for it.

Check to see how the Child is responding to the reparenting. If it can't sense you or isn't taking in your caring, ask why and work with that.

6: Retrieving Your Criticized Child

One of the things the Child may need is to be taken out of the childhood situation.

You can bring it into some place in your present life, your body, or an imaginary place.

7. Unburdening Your Criticized Child

Name the burdens (extreme feelings or beliefs) that the Child is carrying.

Ask the Child if it wants to release the burdens and if it is ready to do so.

If it doesn't want to, ask what it is afraid would happen if it let go of them. Then handle those fears.

How does the Child carry the burdens in or on its body?

What would the Child like to release the burdens to? (light, water, wind, earth, fire, or anything else)

Once the burdens are gone, notice what positive qualities or feelings arise in the Child.

8. Releasing the Critic

See if the Critic is aware of the transformation of the Child. If not, introduce the transformed Child to the Critic.

See if the Critic now realizes that its judgmental role is no longer necessary.

The Critic can choose a new role in your psyche.

(This Help Sheet includes Step 8, even though that step is introduced in the next chapter.)

Summary

In this chapter, you learned how to heal your Criticized Child of its wounds. This sets the stage for helping your Critic to let go of its judgmental role, which we explain in the next chapter.

Chapter 10

Transforming Your Inner Critic

I'm not afraid of storms,
for I'm learning to sail my ship.

—Louisa May Alcott

This chapter shows three ways to help an Inner Critic release its judgmental role. These methods are best used after you have gotten to know the Critic and formed a trusting relationship with it.

Releasing the Critic After Healing the Criticized Child

If you have been following the procedure outlined in this book, you have now done some significant healing with the Criticized Child that the Critic was protecting. Now that the Child is feeling good about herself, the Critic is likely to be able to stop judging you. In most cases, the Critic has been judging you in a misguided attempt to prevent you from acting in ways that would lead to your being judged, attacked, or shamed by your parents. It didn't realize that you are an adult and no longer under their power. However, now that the Child is feeling good about herself, she isn't likely to be so hurt by any new judgments, so the Critic can relax. Furthermore, if someone in the present does judge you and the Child gets hurt, you can now take care of the Child just as you did in the reparenting step. So for all these reasons, the Critic no longer needs to try to protect the Child.

Check with the Critic to see if it is aware of the work you have just done with the Child and how she has been transformed. If not, introduce the Critic to the transformed Child so it can see what has changed in her. You want the Critic to be able to see that the Child is feeling OK now and can't be hurt very much by judgments. Once the Critic recognizes the change in the Child, ask the Critic if it still feels a need to perform its protective role of judging you, or whether it can now let go.[1] Often it will be ready to do this, and it may even be happy to let go of such an onerous job. You may need to discuss any fears it has about letting go and explain how you will handle any judgments that come up in the future.

If your Critic isn't ready to let go of its role, ask what it is concerned would happen if it did. This will give you important information about additional work that may need to be done. Perhaps there are other exiles the Critic is protecting, and it can't let go until they are healed, too. Maybe the Criticized Child is only partially healed, and more work must be done with it. Perhaps the Critic doesn't trust that the Criticized Child is truly healed and needs more time to experience the shift.[2] Other ways to help the Critic feel safe enough to relax and let go are presented later in this chapter.

Once the Critic has let go of its judgmental job, it can choose any other job in your psyche that it wants. It might want to be a supporter for the Child, which means it would become your Inner Champion (see Chapter 11). It might choose a healthier version the job it has been doing, which would make it your Inner Mentor (see Chapter 12). Or it could choose an entirely different role or just decide to take a vacation. When one of Bonnie's clients gets to this stage, she offers the protector the option of joining a

---

1. This is Step 8 of the IFS process, discussed in Chapter 15 of *Self-Therapy*.

2. See Chapter 15 in *Self-Therapy* for other concerns that a protector might have and how to handle them.

wisdom council of parts in the person's psyche, a heart collective, or a grounding team.

Continuation of George's Session

Let's see how this happened in George's session. We pick up at the end of the last chapter when George had finished healing the Little Boy.

George's Inner Critic Cluster

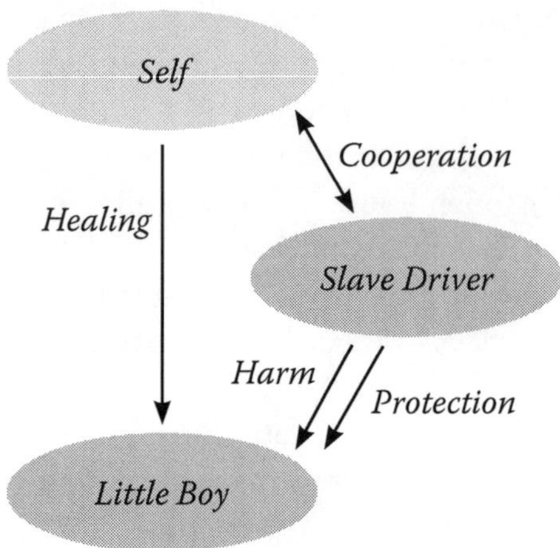

Jay: Now turn your attention back to the Slave Driver. Let me know when you are in touch with it.

George: OK. It see it there.

J: Check to see if it is aware of the work you have just done with the Little Boy and how he has been transformed.

G: Yes. It has been paying attention the whole time. It's kind of amazed that this has happened.

J: Ask the Slave Driver if it might now be willing to let go of judging you.

G: *(pause)* Well, it feels somewhat better, but it is still concerned that I won't work hard enough to be successful.

Critic Realizes That Child Is Transformed

J: Ask the Slave Driver what it is afraid would happen if you didn't work that hard.

G: It is afraid of not getting approval from my boss.

J: Remind the Slave Driver that the Little Boy is feeling fine about himself, so maybe the Slave Driver doesn't need to try so hard to get approval from your boss.

G: It's considering that. *(pause)* Well, it doesn't feel a desperate need for approval anymore, so I can sense that it is relaxing and doesn't have so much charge around this whole thing.

J: Good.

G: But the Slave Driver still isn't ready to completely give up judging. It is afraid of my being lazy and getting bad performance reviews.

The Slave Driver has relaxed some, but more is needed for it to fully transform.

George needs to negotiate with the Slave Driver to let him handle his work from Self, so we will continue with this transcript later in the chapter under Negotiating for Self-Leadership.

Exercise:
Releasing the Critic After Healing the Child

Choose a Criticized Child part that you have healed, as described in the last chapter. Re-access that part and confirm that it is still in the transformed state. Now follow the steps described above to help your Inner Critic release its judgmental role, if it is ready to. Then fill out this sheet.

Transformed Child

____

Critic's concerns about letting go

____

____

How you reassured it

____

____

____

New role it would like to have in your psyche

If you haven't yet healed a Criticized Child, choose one to work on, as described in the previous chapter, and then finish the session by releasing the Critic from its role, as described here.

Example

Let's look at how George filled out the sheet.

Transformed Child

Feeling warm and good about himself.

Critic's concerns about letting go

Worried that I won't work hard and will get judged by my boss.

Introducing the Child to the Critic

In the section above, we discussed introducing the Child to the Critic so the Critic could see how the child has been transformed. However, there is a different use of this introduction that can be a powerful approach to change, even before the Child has been healed. Let's assume that you have gotten to know the Critic and have formed a trusting relationship with it, as described in Chapter 6, but you haven't yet healed the Criticized Child. Perhaps you had a traumatic childhood, so healing the Child will take awhile. Maybe you have an important situation coming up this week in which your Critic is likely to be activated, and you don't have time to go through the healing process with the Child before it happens. Here is a quicker way to release the Critic.

Many Inner Critic parts are paradoxically causing the very pain that they are trying to prevent. In fact, often they are causing far more pain than what they are protecting against. They are stuck in the past, when there was real danger or harm, and they are doing their best to prevent it now. But the only way they know how to do this is to criticize, and they have no clue about the pain this is causing. Therefore we can change the situation by making them aware of the impact of their criticism. Recall the doctor in Chapter 8 who bled his patients. If someone explained to him about germs and hygiene, this would wake him up to the problems he was causing.

First access the Criticized Child and get to know it, as described in the beginning of Chapter 8. You especially want to get clear on how the Child has been hurt by the Inner Critic's attacks and how it is continuing to be hurt by the Critic. Then introduce the Child to the Inner Critic so the Critic becomes aware of how it has been harming the Child. Ask the Critic if it was aware of the pain it was causing the Child.

Your Critic might say something like, "Oh my gosh. I didn't know I was causing pain. That's not what I intended. I was just trying to help you not be judged by people." Ask the Critic how it feels now that it knows this. It may say that it is sorry to be hurting the Child.

In some cases, the Critic is not only causing the Child pain, but it is also producing the very behavior in the Child that it is trying to prevent. For example, an Inner Controller Critic might be trying to prevent the Child from overeating by judging it. However, its judgments will make the Child feel ashamed and depressed, which may cause it to turn to food to dull the pain. You can ask the Critic to notice that it is causing this behavior in the Child. This information will give it even more motivation to stop its attacks. Now ask the Critic if it might be willing to relax and decrease its judgments. It will often agree.

If it isn't ready to shift, ask the Critic what it is afraid would happen if it let go of judging. It may still feel that its protection is necessary. When you find out what it is afraid of, reassure it about these concerns (see the next section). If the Critic is willing, see if it wants to choose another role in your psyche or if it just wants to modulate its statements to a more benign form.

Critic Realizes It is Causing Child Pain

Introducing the Child to the Critic is useful either before or after the Child has been healed (or partially healed). Sometimes the Inner Critic can't let go of its judgmental role very easily, even after the Child has been healed. In this case, showing the wounded Child to the Critic can facilitate this process.

This introduction doesn't work with all Critics. Some already know that they are harming the Child. For example, some Critics hurt the Child purposely to undermine your self-confidence so you won't take risks that they think are dangerous. For these Critics, this introduction won't be effective.

Exercise: Introducing the Child to the Critic

Choose a Critic to work with that you already have a trusting relationship with. Access the Criticized Child that is being harmed by it, as described above.

Image of the Child

____

Child's feelings and beliefs

____

____

How Child is being harmed by Critic

____

____

Introduce the Critic to the Child and find out if the Critic knew it was harming the Child

____

How the Critic responds to knowing that it is causing the Child pain

____

____

Is the Critic now ready to let go of criticizing?

____

If not, what it is concerned about

If so, new role for Critic or new form of its statements

Example

Image of the Child

5 year old hiding his face in corner

Child's feelings and beliefs

He is not interesting or valuable because he is not intellectual.

How Child is being harmed by

Critic Critic tells him no one cares about him because he is dumb.

Introduce the Critic to the Child and find out if the Critic knew it was harming the Child

No

How the Critic responds to knowing that it is causing the Child pain

Surprise and chagrin

Is the Critic now ready to let go of criticizing?

Maybe

If not, what it is concerned about

Critic wants me to be more intellectual so I can make intelligent conversation and be liked.

Negotiating for Self-Leadership

Here is another approach to releasing the Critic that doesn't depend on healing the Criticized Child first. Now that you are beginning to have a connection with your Critic, it may be able to cooperate with you and learn a different way to respond when a situation triggers it. When a situation arises that activates your Critic, such as writing a paper, going out on a date, or interviewing for a job, it usually starts pushing and attacking you. You can learn to negotiate with it to allow *you* to take the lead in these situations. Explain to your Critic that because you are in Self, you can handle this situation and make good decisions. The Critic doesn't have to use its judgmental strategy to protect you because you don't need as much protection, and you have a better way of handling difficult situations. Since you have developed a trusting relationship with your Critic, it is likely to listen to you now.

Your Inner Critic became extreme in childhood because it was dealing with a dangerous or harmful situation, for example, being ridiculed when you tried to get attention or always being told that your work wasn't good enough. And it believes that the same harm is going to happen now in your current adult life. Furthermore, when you were little, there wasn't a mature Self there to help, so the Critic had to handle this painful state of affairs all on its own.

Now that you are an adult, you have a competent, perceptive Self to help in difficult circumstances. Or perhaps you haven't had very much access to your Self, but it is now starting to become available because you are reading this book, doing this IFS work, and learning to access it. However, your Critic doesn't realize that your Self is now available to help, so you need to make this clear. Since your Self and your Critic are now connected, the Critic is more likely to listen to you and trust what you say.

In childhood, you were attacked, rejected, or shamed for some reason. However, from the place of Self, you can explain to the Critic that the current situation is very different from what happened then. You are no longer vulnerable and dependent like a child. You are autonomous and are no longer under the power of your parents. You have many strengths and capacities as an adult (possibly because of previous work you have done on yourself) that you didn't have as a child. For example, you are more grounded and centered. You may be more assertive, more perceptive about interpersonal situations, better able to support yourself financially, and so on. You have already accomplished things in your life and overcome various obstacles. You are an adult with much greater ability to handle yourself. You have friends, maybe a spouse or lover, perhaps a community you belong to, a support group, or professionals you can rely on. You have people you can turn to, if necessary.

This means that you aren't in danger the way you were as a child, and your mature Self is available, which wasn't possible when you were little. Therefore, your Critic can relax and allow you to handle things. You can explain to the Critic how you will handle any situations that come up now that it might be worried about. Ask it to trust you and allow you to be in charge of these circumstances.

In this illustration, the Critic believes that it is the Child who is going to a job interview and therefore she will fail. The Self reassures the Critic that she (the Self) can handle the interview successfully and asks the Critic to allow her to do that.

If your Critic relaxes, there may be certain healthy capacities that it could bring to these situations, and you could help it do that. If this is so, explain to your Critic how it can help in a healthy way.

Let's look at an example of this negotiating process.

Self Reassures Critic About Handing Situation

Negotiating for Self-Leadership with the Perfectionist

One type of Inner Critic is the Perfectionist, which demands that your work be perfect and attacks you when it thinks it isn't. Sometimes a Perfectionist will keep you from writing, performing, or producing anything, even if no one will see it. This Critic especially tends to be activated when you are learning a skill or when you are experimenting in a creative way with something new. The Perfectionist is afraid to let you come up with or produce anything because it may not be very good at first, and that is frightening for this

Perfectionist Critic Causes Writer's Block

part. You were harshly criticized or shamed in the past, and the Perfectionist is trying to prevent this from happening again. This Critic is the cause of writer's block for many people.

Let's look at how you might negotiate with this type of Perfectionist Critic. There are two possibilities:

1. No one will see what you produce. In this case, you can explain to the Perfectionist that you are safe from criticism. Initially, you will be producing work that may not be very good, but that is to be expected, and it may even be necessary for your learning or experimentation. Your work is just a rough draft and will be improved or even rewritten many times as you go. Therefore you don't have to worry about its quality at all. You won't show your work to anyone until you have improved it to the point at which it is very good, and therefore you will be safe.

2. You will be showing your work to a teacher, a colleague, or someone else. In this case, you can explain to the Perfectionist that these people know that your work is at an early stage or that you are just learning or experimenting. They don't expect you to be excellent yet. If they do criticize your work, it is only aimed at helping you learn or improve what you are doing. Therefore, the Perfectionist can relax and allow you to operate without being

concerned about your output. Remind the Critic that these people aren't your parents or grade-school teachers (or whoever originally criticized you).

Even if one of these people **is** harsh, and you end up being judged or even shamed for what you produce, you can handle that. You are resilient and self-supporting; you won't fall apart. You have much more internal strength for dealing with this situation than you did as a child. You have friends and colleagues to turn to now.

Your Perfectionist *does* have an important role to play in helping you to improve your work, but its input must come at the right time, which is after you have produced something that is far enough along for evaluation to be useful. Then the Perfectionist,

Healthy Role for Perfectionist

like a good coach, can criticize what you have done and help you to improve it. If you are writing, this shouldn't happen after each sentence but instead at the end, when you have finished what you are producing. Then its input will be helpful. If you are in the early stages of a project, or if you are just learning a skill or are experimenting with something new, a critique probably isn't called for yet. It will be needed later on, when your work is somewhat polished. Most important, by holding off until then, the critique won't get in the way of your learning or creativity. By working this way, your Perfectionist has become an Inner Mentor (see Chapter 12).

Ask your Perfectionist if it would be willing to take the chance to let you produce work without criticism and see what happens. Ask it to let you (in Self) be in charge, and reassure it that there isn't much danger and that you can handle whatever may happen. You are asking it to allow you to take the lead. You will then let it know when is the right time for the Perfectionist to bring in its critical skills in a helpful way. It is more likely to agree to this because you have already connected with it and it trusts you.

This is one example of how negotiating for Self-leadership can be done. You will need to adapt this to whatever type of Critic you have and the kinds of situations that trigger it.

Negotiating for Self-leadership can be useful either before or after the Criticized Child has been healed. It provides additional reassurance for the Critic to relax its judgmental role.

Negotiating with George's Critic

We will now continue with George's session from earlier in this chapter. This section illustrates one form of negotiating for Self-leadership.

George: But the Slave Driver still isn't ready to completely give up judging. He is afraid of my being lazy and getting bad reviews from my boss.

Jay: Let me check on something. Have you actually been working adequately on the project at your job? Consider this question from Self, not from the Slave Driver's perspective.

I want to find out if the Slave Driver's fear of George not working well is valid or whether it is an outmoded childhood fear, so I check with George in Self to see what the reality is.

G: For the most part, I have been working well. Occasionally I procrastinate. Usually that's because I'm afraid that I won't do a job well enough, when there's a feeling of inadequacy.

J: Is it the Little Boy who feels inadequate?

G: Hmm. That's an interesting question. (pause) Yes. It is that part. That's what throws me off. And then a procrastinating part comes in to try to avoid feeling inadequate by not trying at all.

J: So explain to the Slave Driver that this isn't so likely to happen now that the Boy is feeling good about himself.

Now that the Boy is healed, there isn't the same need for protection from the Slave Driver. My suggestion is aimed at helping it realize that.

G: The Slave Driver is listening and seems to be relaxing some.

J: And if the Slave Driver stops judging you, the Little Boy can continue to feel confident. In fact, explain to the Slave Driver that its judgments have been part of the problem.

This is similar to what we did in the previous section when we introduced the Critic to the Child so the Critic could see the harm it had been causing.

G: It's really thinking about that. It is shocked to even consider that. *(pause)* Well, it's trusting me a lot more now, so it's willing to consider that it should stop judging me. But it's still worried about my not working hard enough.

J: Explain to it that you agree with its goal of working hard in order to do a good job. Remind it that you have been working well most of the time, and that, as an adult, you have good work capacities.

Since the Slave Driver still has concerns, we must address them, one at a time. Here we explain that George has the capacity to work well when in Self.

G: I'm telling it that I can plan my work, pace myself, keep up my motivation, and ask for help when I need it. And I commit myself to working well, so it doesn't need to push me. *(pause)* It likes that idea, but it's still worried about getting judged by my boss.

J: OK. Remind the Slave Driver that you aren't a child anymore, and you're no longer under your father's power.

G: I also told it that my boss is pretty reasonable most of the time, unlike my father.

J: Good. You could also explain to the Slave Driver that if your boss does judge you and it hurts the Little Boy, you will take care of the Boy just like you did earlier in the session, so he will end up feeling good about himself.

Here we are addressing more concerns of the Slave Driver.

G: I'm also telling the Slave Driver that if my boss does get unreasonable, I will talk to him about how he is treating you. I won't just put up with it. (pause) That makes the Slave Driver feel better. It says it's willing to try this approach and see if it works.

J: Great! Thank it for that.

We have finally addressed the Slave Driver's worries enough that it is willing to experiment with allowing the Self to lead.

Exercise: Negotiating for Self-Leadership

Choose a Critic to work with that you already understand and have a good relationship with.

Image of Critic

____

What it says to you

____

What situations trigger it

What it is trying to protect you from

Childhood fears of Critic

Why those fears aren't valid now

What resources you bring to the situation now

____

____

How you will handle the situation in a way that is effective

____

____

____

What the Critic can offer the situation in a healthy way

____

____

____

Example

Let's look at how George filled out the answers for this exercise.

What it is trying to protect you from

Being judged by my boss

Childhood fears of Critic

My father being angry at him about doing homework

Why those fears aren't valid now

I'm no longer a child under my father's power.

My boss is more reasonable than my father was.

What resources you bring to the situation now

The capacity and commitment to work well.

How you will handle the situation in a way that is effective

I will work well, and if the boss does judge me, I will take care of the Child's feelings.

What the Critic can offer the situation in a healthy way

Not there yet, but willing to let me lead.

Help Sheet 3: Transforming Your Critic

You can refer to this Help Sheet while you are working on yourself to guide your steps.

It can also be used when you are facilitating a partner.

Introducing the Criticized Child to the Inner Critic

Access the Criticized Child.

Understand its pain, especially how it gets hurt by the Critic.

Introduce the Child to the Critic.

Ask the Critic if it realized it was hurting the Child.

Ask the Critic if it is ready to let go of its judgmental role.

If necessary, reassure it about any concerns it has about letting go.

Critic chooses new role.

Negotiating for Self-Leadership

Describe to the Critic what your capacities are as an adult in Self.

Explain to the Critic why the current life situations it is concerned about are not as dangerous as when you were young.

Tell it what you intend to do in these situations to handle them safely.

Ask the Critic to relax and let you lead in these situations.

If appropriate, explain to the Critic how it can aid you in a healthy way.

Summary

In this chapter, you have learned three methods for helping an Inner Critic part to transform. (1) Showing it the transformed Child and seeing if it no longer needs to protect it. (2) Showing the Critic how much it is harming the Child and seeing if it wants to stop doing that. (3) Negotiating with the Critic to allow you (in Self) to handle a situation that the Critic is concerned about. In the next chapter, we go on to evoke your Inner Champion to help support you in the face of Inner Critic attacks.

Chapter 11

Awakening Your Inner Champion

> The only service a friend can really render is to keep your courage by holding up to you a mirror in which you can see a noble image of yourself
>
> —*George Bernard Shaw*

The Inner Champion is an aspect of the Self that supports us and helps us to feel good about ourselves. It encourages us to be who we truly are rather than fitting into the box our Inner Critic creates for us. It is a magic bullet for dealing with the negative impacts of your Inner Critic. One way to think about your Inner Champion is that it is the ideal supportive parent that you always wished you had. It is an aspect of the IFS Self that responds in a helpful way to Inner Critic messages. This chapter will help you get in touch with your Champion so you can evoke it when you need it in the face of an Inner Critic attack.

If it feels frightening to you to evoke an Inner Champion, feel free to skip this chapter. You can free yourself from your Inner Critic without it.

George's Inner Champion

George learned to evoke his Inner Champion when his Slave Driver Critic was judging him and pushing him to work harder. Here is what his Champion said to him:

"You can trust yourself to do a good job at work.

I accept you just the way you are.

You can accomplish what is needed in a stress-free way.

You have the right to a relaxed work life.

You can be a very successful and valued employee without killing yourself.

You have the right to work reasonable hours so you can enjoy the rest of your life."

This helped George to feel confident and relaxed at work and to have time for his family and leisure activities.

George's Inner Champion

Inner Champion Statements

Our Inner Champions can help us in four different ways— boundary setting, nurturing, guidance, and action planning. Let's look at each of these aspects of the Champion with examples of statements it can make.

Boundary Setting with the Critic

Your Inner Champion can set limits on your Inner Critic when this is necessary to get you some space to feel yourself and take stock. It can make statements to your Inner Critic such as the following:

Your judgments aren't helpful.

Now is not a good time for this.

Your judgments are making it more difficult for me.

Please step aside right now; your attitude is causing problems.

I know you want to protect me, but your approach isn't working.

I know your heart is in the right place. Let me show you a more effective way to accomplish your goals.

Nurturing

Your Inner Champion can make supportive, nurturing statements to you that help you to accept and appreciate yourself. For example:

I completely accept you no matter what.

I love you.

I care about you.

You have accomplished many valuable things in your life.

I appreciate your qualities and capacities.

You have a lot to offer people and the world.

You are special to me.

I value you just for being you.

You are beautiful and whole just the way you are.
You already are everything you need to be right now.

Guidance

Your Inner Champion can make encouraging statements to help guide you on your way and support you to move ahead in your life.

You can trust yourself.

Your struggles just represent where you are now in your growth.

You can do it.

I support you in whatever you take on.

You are doing well. You are on your way.

I want you to have your heart's desire in life.

I'm proud of you.

You will find a way forward.

You will discover what it is you are meant to do.

You have the right to be yourself and do things your way.

Action Planning

Your Inner Champion can make suggestions to help you plan actions you need to take.

You have the right to take your time and do things at your own pace.

Congratulations on accomplishing that step.

You can overcome whatever obstacles are in your path.

You can find supportive people in your life.

You can correct course whenever necessary; that doesn't mean you have failed.

You can use the application on our website (see Appendix B) to profile an Inner Champion for you in response to each of the seven Critics. You have an opportunity to profile what you want your personal Champion to say to you and what it looks like, from each of its four aspects.

A Healthy Version of the Inner Defender

In Chapter 5, we introduced the Inner Defender. This is the part of you that argues with your Inner Critic and tries to convince it that you really are a good person. It may fight with the Critic over its judgments of you—for example, "You're wrong. I *am* adequate. Look at all the things I have accomplished in my life." This part is attempting to counter the Inner Critic in an adversarial way. However, this creates inner conflict because the Critic will fight back, which can't be a good solution.

The Inner Champion is the healthy version of the Inner Defender. It doesn't fight with the Inner Critic, though it may set some limits on the Critic. The main thing it does is to support you (and your Criticized Child) in the face of the Critic's attacks. It helps you to feel self-confident, not by fighting with the Critic but by supporting and encouraging you. This way doesn't promote inner discord.

Seven Flavors of Inner Champions

Since our Inner Champion helps us deal with our Inner Critic, there is a specific version of the Inner Champion for each of the seven types of Critics. We will examine each one.

These descriptions are intended to inspire you with possibilities, not to limit or define your experience. Feel free to allow these helpful aspects of yourself to emerge in whatever way is unique to you.

Perfectionist

In the face of a Perfectionist Critic, your Inner Champion supports your right to *not* be perfect. It reminds you that it is only human to make mistakes, and making an error doesn't mean that there is anything wrong with you. It reminds you that you are totally OK

Perfectionist Inner Champion

even if you don't get everything right. It supports your right to have balance in your life—to rest, take care of yourself, and enjoy life. It knows that many jobs just need to be done well enough, not to super-high standards. It has the wisdom to know that sometimes it is important to go with the flow and let things evolve rather than trying to get everything perfect right away. It supports you in being a learner who doesn't have to know everything to start with. It knows the meaning of "rough draft."

Underminer

An Underminer Critic tries to make you feel inadequate so you won't take risks that it considers dangerous. In response, your Inner Champion can discriminate when there is real danger and when there isn't. It understands that you have many more resources, both inner and outer, available to you than when you were a child. It knows that you have inner strength and resilience, that you have people to help and support you. So it realizes that

Underminer Inner Champion

you can handle most difficulties that arise from taking risks or being powerful. Furthermore, it can recognize when you are in a situation that *isn't* dangerous, in which you are unlikely to be attacked for being large and visible. Therefore, it knows that you can venture out and succeed. It holds a vision of you being powerful and innovative and making your mark on the world.

Taskmaster

If you have a Taskmaster Critic, your Inner Champion has a two-pronged attitude: It supports you to work hard and accomplish things, and it also recognizes that you are just fine the way you are. Although this may sound paradoxical, this kind of self-acceptance actually supports you in developing yourself. Your Champion encourages you to succeed in a relaxed, easygoing way. It doesn't expect you to overwork or to be relentless in achieving your goals. Yet it knows that you can achieve what you set out to do.

Taskmaster Inner Champion

Inner Controller

An Inner Controller Critic judges you harshly to try to stop you from overeating, using drugs, or indulging in other dangerous ways. In response, your Champion tells you that your needs and desires are OK and that you are fine just as you are. It supports you in being relaxed and trusting of your decisions about what you eat or what you do. It also supports you in being centered and in touch with your body, which naturally brings moderation. It supports your capacity for healthy pleasure and sensuality in life, which is satisfying enough that there is no need for overindulgence.

Inner Controler Inner Champion

Guilt Tripper Inner Champion

Guilt Tripper

With a Guilt Tripper Critic, your Inner Champion supports you in feeling good about yourself in the face of guilt. When you examine your true values, if you feel that what you did wasn't wrong, like leaving home or marrying someone you love who is of a different race or religion, the Inner Champion supports you in not feeling guilty about it. It tells you that you were acting in integrity and that you are a good person. It tells the Guilt Tripper to back off because its outmoded values came from your family or culture and don't reflect your truth.

Molder

A Molder Critic tries to get you to be a certain way based on the values of your parents or culture. In response, your Inner Champion helps you to see that the Molder's values are not the only good way to live your life. It supports you in determining your own choices of lifestyle and way of being. It tells you that you are a good person even if you choose to live your life in a way that goes against your upbringing and culture. Your Champion supports you in being yourself and living according to your deepest values. It

Molder Inner Champion

wants you to actualize your true nature and live according to your highest calling, whether or not this fits any external idea of what is right.

Destroyer

In the face of a Destroyer Critic, your Inner Champion affirms that you have the right to exist. It is your birthright. Your Inner Champion loves you and cares for you. She has great compassion for your suffering and wants you to feel good and whole. She holds you close and tells you that you are precious to her. She nurtures you in the most fundamental bodily way, not only because you need it but also because she loves to be close to you.

Destroyer Inner Champion

Sometimes the Destroyer Critic turns anger or aggression inward toward you that was originally meant for other people in the outside world. Your Inner Champion can redirect it to where it belongs. It affirms that you have the right to be angry at people who have hurt you or neglected you, to set limits, to protect yourself, or to be powerful. And yes, this may involve ending a job or relationship that isn't right for you.

It may seem, from these descriptions, that your Inner Champion is being too easy on you and isn't helping you to look at issues of yours that need to be worked on. This is because that is the job of your Inner Mentor, which we will explore in the next chapter.

Exercise: Awakening Your Inner Champion

Your Inner Champion is a natural part of your Self—who you really are. You can often get in touch with it just by tuning in to that place in you that we have described. However, it can also be built on a foundation of past moments in your life, drawing on people who have championed you, who really saw you and heard you, who recognized you and had faith in you. You can draw the Champion's wisdom from people you admired as they lived their lives with integrity. You can remember people who were kind and supportive to others, people who held far-reaching visions for themselves and those they loved. Who have been your Champions?

Find a quiet place to sit and relax. You might play some gentle, evocative music. Ground yourself by breathing deeply in your belly, feeling your feet on the floor, your back on the chair, your shoulders relaxed, your jaw slightly open.

You are going to take a trip back in time. Look for moments when you felt seen, appreciated, acknowledged. You could start from early childhood and work your way up to the present or go backward from the present time. Let the memories of these moments come as they will—images, sensations, smells, feelings.

Remember a time when you were recognized, encouraged, or supported by someone. A wise person may have stood up for you, guided you, or just let you know that they saw your pain. This support may have come from a teacher, coach, neighbor, friend, parent, or friend's parent.

You can also look for figures from books, TV, or the movies—someone you admired for their ability to champion others, for example, the trainer's faith in *Rocky*, the spirited trio in the movie *Nine to Five*, the father in *Father Knows Best*. Or you may find strong images from mythology—Athena, Mercury, Artemis, Gandalf. You may be drawn to a famous person, such as Gandhi, Margaret Mead, Nelson Mandela, Oprah Winfrey, Amelia Earhart, Winston Churchill, Rachel Carson, Barack Obama, Gloria Steinem, Paul Newman, Katharine Hepburn, Georgia O'Keeffe, or Michael Jordan.

As you find figures to inspire your Inner Champion, ask them to step over to your side, to be on your team, to surround you with their strength. They will help you in dealing with your Inner Critics and moving forward in your life.

Exercise: Inner Champion Statements

In this exercise, you will be crafting statements that you want your Inner Champion to say to you. These might be statements that you already hear from inside or ones that you are beginning to hear more often. Or they can simply be statements that you would like to hear from an Inner Champion, even if this has never happened.

Remember that your Inner Champion always supports you. It doesn't tell you what to do or not do. It tells you what you *can* do or what you have *the right* to do. It doesn't say, "Don't give up"—it says, "You can succeed if you stay with it." It doesn't say, "Take it easy"—it says, "You have the right to take it easy." It makes personal statements directly to you. Rather than saying, "You are lovable," it says, "I love you."

Now consider a situation in which your Inner Critic gets activated and attacks you.

___

___

You will be invoking your Inner Champion to support you in the face of those attacks. Think about what you would like to hear from your Inner Champion in this situation. What do you want it to say to you?

___

___

___

___

___

Consider when this situation is likely to happen over the next week or two.

___

___

___

Be aware during these times if your Inner Critic gets activated. If it is helpful, evoke the image (or images) of your Inner Champion from the previous exercise. Imagine this figure saying the above Inner Champion statements to you. How does that make you feel?

____

____

____

Example

Here is what one person wrote for this exercise.

Now consider a situation in which your Inner Critic gets activated and attacks you.

Giving a talk at work.

You will be invoking your Inner Champion to support you in the face of those attacks. Think about what you would like to hear from your Inner Champion in this situation. What do you want it to say to you?

You can do it.

I appreciate your creative ideas.

People will be interested in what you have to say.

They want you to succeed because that means they will learn something.

I care for you and support you no matter what happens.

Consider when this situation is likely to happen over the next week or two.

Project report on Wednesday.

Be aware during these time if your Inner Critic gets activated. Then evoke the image (or images) of your Inner Champion from the previous exercise. Imagine this figure saying the above Inner Champion statements to you. How does that make you feel?

Calmer and more confident.

Summary

In this chapter, you learned to evoke your Inner Champion to support you in the face of your Inner Critic, and how to apply this to specific situations in your life. In the next chapter, we will explore your Inner Mentor—the healthy version of your Inner Critic.

Chapter 12

Your Inner Mentor

I am not discouraged, because
every wrong attempt discarded is another step forward.

—Thomas Alva Edison

Our Inner Critics are trying to perform a function that is necessary in our psyches. We all need the ability to look at ourselves realistically to see how we could change and improve. We want to be aware of the ways we act that don't align with our values. We need to be able to see when we are hurting someone unnecessarily or when we aren't working to our potential. We must recognize when we are doing something dangerous or compromising to our health, when we are being shortsighted because of a need for immediate gratification. The problem is that the Inner Critic performs this function in a way that undermines our self-esteem and self-confidence. Sometimes it criticizes us in ways that are simply false and totally unnecessary. However, there are times when there is a grain of truth in the judgments of our Critic, or even when a judgment contains wisdom we have been ignoring. In these cases, the problem isn't the content of the Critic's judgment but rather the harsh, nasty, condemning way it is delivered. The message doesn't have to be expressed this way; there is another option.

Your Inner Mentor

It is possible to have a gentler and wiser voice inside that we call the *Inner Mentor*. This is really a healthy version of the Critic. It performs this necessary function in our psyches in a positive way, whereas the Critic does it in a destructive way.

Let's see how this might work by looking at an example. Suppose you are a parent, and your child doesn't clean up his room the way you asked him to. If you act like an Inner Critic, you might say in a harsh, loud voice, "What a mess! You're so dumb. Can't you do anything right?" However, if you instead act like an Inner Mentor, you might say in a kindly, supportive voice, "Honey, that's not quite what I was looking for. Let me show you how to clean up a room. Let's do it together."

Recall Jill from Chapter 2 who was nervous before a date and binged on cake. Her Critic screamed at her, "You look fat! No man will ever marry you." Suppose that instead of her Critic saying those things, her Inner Mentor had said, "Okay, that wasn't the best response to the nervousness you were feeling. It would be better to stay with your feelings than to overeat, but I know that is hard. I will help you forgive yourself and find a better way next time." Then Jill wouldn't have spent the next 24 hours worrying about her date. She could have been confident and excited and had a good time over dinner.

This is how your Inner Mentor can treat you—with love and acceptance. It can also help you be clear about how you acted that wasn't aligned with who you want to be, and it will help you take action to remedy the situation.

George's Inner Mentor

When the Inner Critic transforms, it often becomes the Inner Mentor because the Mentor is a healthy version of the Critic. Recall that George had a Slave Driver Critic, which constantly judged him and pushed him to work harder. When the Slave Driver transformed, it became a kind coach.

George's Slave Driver Transforms into His Inner Mentor

Before

After

George's Inner Mentor said, "Most of the time you work quite well, but every once in a while you procrastinate on a project and it gets you in trouble. You don't need to work harder, you just need to notice when you are avoiding a task so you can get back on track.

I will help you do that. It seems to happen when you're feeling insecure about a job you have to do. Then you start playing games on your computer and reading the news too much. When that happens, I will signal you so you realize what is happening. Then I'll help you face the job you have been avoiding. This will not only get you better reviews from your boss, it will also make your life easier because you won't be forced to pull an all-nighter every once in a while. I will also help you use IFS to work on that procrastinator part and the insecure exile it is protecting. I will remind you of this at your next session." This helps George to overcome his problem with procrastination without undermining his self-confidence in any way.

Your Inner Mentor and Inner Champion

You need both your Inner Mentor and your Inner Champion in order to feel good about yourself and function well. They naturally and easily work together. Your Inner Champion supports you in feeling good about yourself and moving ahead in your life. Your Inner Mentor helps you to see where you can improve yourself.

For example, suppose you lost it and yelled at your daughter, making her upset. A Guilt Tripper Inner Critic might castigate you, saying, "You are a horrible parent. How could you do that terrible thing to her? And you've done it so many times before. You don't deserve to have such a wonderful child. You are ruining her life. You should be shot!" Your Inner Champion might say, "I know you're really a good mother. Everyone gets angry occasionally. You really love her and want the best for her. Pick up the pieces and move on from here." This is the support you need, especially in the face of an attack from your Guilt Tripper.

However, this isn't all you need. You also need a constructive voice to help you look at what went wrong and what you can do about it. Your Inner Mentor might say, "I know that's not the way you want to treat your daughter, because you love her. Let's see what you can do to keep this from happening again. Your life has been very stressful lately, and you need to take better care of yourself. You could notice when you are starting to get angry with her and remember not to take it out on her. You could explore what's behind your anger, which may have nothing to do with her. You could take a brief time-out when you find yourself starting to lose control." Your Inner Mentor would say this in a kindly, helpful manner, without judgment.

So you can see that the Inner Champion and Inner Mentor are a great pair. They each supply something important. They each support a key healthy capacity in you. The Inner Champion supports your capacity for self-esteem, and the Inner Mentor supports your capacity for self-improvement. Recall in last chapter we saw that the Inner Champion is a healthy version of the Inner Defender. The Inner Mentor is a healthy version of the Inner Critic.

We can now look at a full version of the Inner Critic cluster, including these healthy parts. The Inner Champion is above the

George Supported by His Inner Champion and Inner Mentor

Inner Defender in the graphic, showing that one is a healthy version of the other. And the Inner Mentor is above the Inner Critic for the same reason.

Inner Critic Cluster

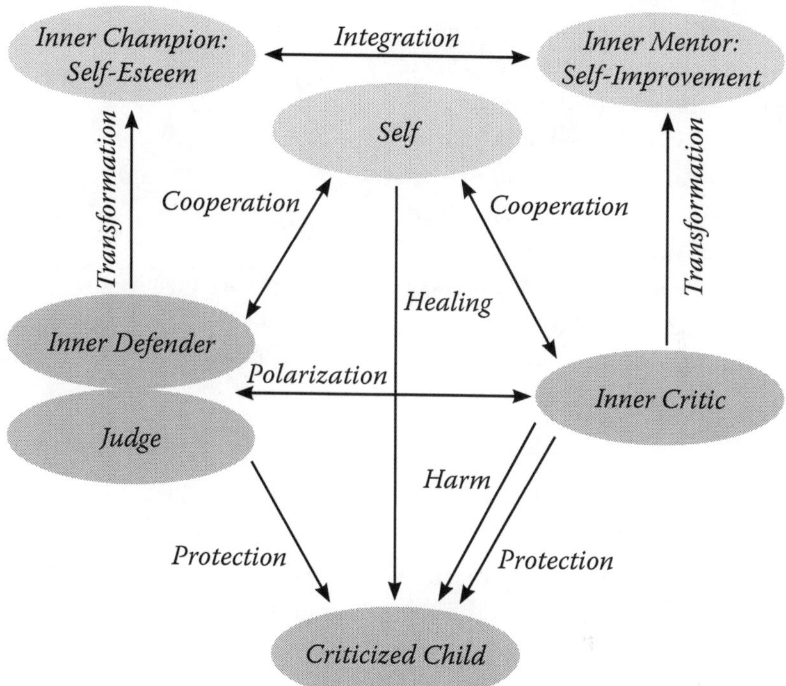

In some situations, the Inner Mentor is not needed. Sometimes your Inner Critic judges you about something that is just plain false; there is no grain of truth in its accusation. For example, the Critic says you are worthless and will never amount to anything. Then you only need your Inner Champion to support your self-esteem. There is no need for you to change anything.

In IFS terms, the Inner Champion and Inner Mentor can be seen as aspects of Self or as parts in their natural, healthy state. They manifest healthy qualities that intrinsically exist in you unless they are blocked, usually by the

Inner Critic. In this sense, they are aspects of Self. However, when the Inner Critic transforms and chooses a new job in your psyche, it often chooses to become the Inner Mentor, since that is the healthy version of the Critic. And the Inner Defender can transform into the Inner Champion. In these cases, the Mentor and Champion would be seen as healthy parts. In our view, all healthy parts can be seen as more delineated, personified aspects of Self, so there is no need to choose between these two perspectives. We see the Champion and Mentor as both healthy parts and as aspects of Self.

Mentor and Champion as Aspects of Self (Heart)

Seven Types of Inner Mentors

We have delineated a specific version of the Inner Mentor for each of the seven types of Inner Critics. Each Mentor embodies a certain wisdom for dealing with these seven issues in your life. Let's look at each in turn.

Taskmaster Inner Mentor

If you have been procrastinating or not working enough to get what you want in life, your Taskmaster Inner Mentor will help you, in a kindly, supportive way, to see that something needs to change. It will aid you in devising a work plan that can be successful. It will encourage you to work on the parts in you that are avoiding tasks that need to be done. It also recognizes that goals change over time, and it is flexible in what it expects from you while still gently encouraging you to do more.

Perfectionist Inner Mentor

Your Perfectionist Inner Mentor can differentiate between a situation in which your current efforts are enough for your purposes and one in which you really do need to improve. If you have a part that tends to be too loose or turn in work that is incomplete, your Inner Mentor will help you see that more effort is required, and it will do this in a supportive, encouraging way.

Inner Controller Inner Mentor

If you really are indulging in a dangerous way, your Inner Mentor will remind you about this in a caring way. It will help you to devise a plan for controlling your appetites in a way that is flexible and realistic. It can help you find a venue where you can work with your Indulger part, discover the underlying needs that are triggering it, and change its behavior—perhaps a 12-step program or an IFS therapist.

Guilt Tripper Inner Mentor

If you did something that went against your true values or caused harm that you regret, your Inner Mentor knows that it is important to take responsibility for your actions. It finds a supportive way to help you own up to your actions and their consequences. It helps you to make amends for what you did and set it right. If necessary, it helps you to work on and transform the parts of you that took those actions so they won't happen again. All this is done by your Inner Mentor without making you feel bad about yourself.

Molder Inner Mentor

If you tend to get into trouble because you ignore conventional ways of doing things, your Inner Mentor can point this out in a caring way. If you have a Rebel part that needs to defy tradition just for the sake of defiance, your Inner Mentor can recognize this part and help you work with it to relax its extreme defiance so you can discover your true inner values.

Underminer Inner Mentor

If you are in a situation in which being visible could realistically be risky, your Mentor can advise you of this from a rational place and help you decide how to handle the problem. If you are considering trying something that you may not succeed at because of your limitations, your Inner Mentor will help you to evaluate this without judgment. It will help you to be realistic about both your strengths and limitations and choose a way to step out into the world that will be satisfying.

Destroyer

Because the Destroyer tends to be so harmful, we haven't seen situations in which a Destroyer Inner Mentor is called for. What is needed is a strong Inner Champion (see Chapter 11).

These descriptions are intended to inspire you with possibilities, not to limit or define your experience. Feel free to allow these helpful aspects of yourself to emerge in whatever way is unique to you.

Exercise: Evoking Your Inner Mentor

Think of a situation that tends to trigger your Inner Critic where there is some truth to its judgment of you. The situation

____

What the Critic says to you

____

____

Evoke your Inner Champion, as we described last chapter, to support you in feeling better about yourself and knowing that you don't deserve to be treated in a harsh way. What does it says to you?

____

____

____

Now think about how you would like your Inner Mentor to help you with the situation. Its input will usually be a paragraph of advice and ideas, not just a series of statements. Write this here.

____

____

____

____

____

Example

Think of a situation that tends to trigger your Inner Critic where there is some truth to its judgment of you. The situation

Yelled at my daughter and upset her.

What the Critic says to you

You are a horrible parent. How could you do that terrible thing to her? And you've done it so many times before. You are ruining her life!

Evoke your Inner Champion, as we described last chapter, to support you in feeling better about yourself and knowing that you don't deserve to be treated in a harsh way. What does it says to you?

I know you're really a good mother. Everyone gets angry occasionally. You really love her and want the best for her. Pick up the pieces and move on from here.

Now think about how you would like your Inner Mentor to help you with the situation. Its input will usually be a paragraph of advice and ideas, not just a series of statements. Write this here.

I know that's not the way you want to treat your daughter, because you love her. Let's see what you can do to keep this from happening again. Your life has been very stressful lately, and you need to take better care of yourself. You could notice when you are starting to get angry with her and remember not to take it out on her. You could explore what's behind your anger, which may have nothing to do with her.

Summary

In this chapter, you learned about your Inner Mentor and how it is different from your Inner Champion. You explored the seven types of Inner Mentors and practiced evoking your Mentor in a real-life situation.

Chapter 13

Conclusion

We cannot give any reason for the fact that we love being ourselves. We can come up with reasons, but none of them will be true because there aren't any; we just inherently love ourselves and our nature. And in our True Nature, we love everything and everybody. That love is simply part of reality.

—A. H. Almaas,
The Unfolding Now

Being Free of Your Inner Critics

When you have worked with your Inner Critic parts and your Criticized Child parts enough that they are healed and transformed, what will your life be like? What is it like to be free of your Inner Critics?

There is an amazing reinforcing quality that happens when you walk away from old patterns of self-hatred. Like taking the first tentative steps on stones across a stream, you find your footing and dance lightly ahead. You no longer have to rely on the tattered net of old beliefs to hold you. Your safety net becomes a newly woven fabric of self-confidence and self-love loomed from inner support, experiences of successful living, and your growing capacities.

One of the participants in our Inner Critic Class says, "I learned that while my Inner Critic can give me harsh messages to shy away from situations, she really means to protect me from my personal pain, fear, and grief. So I embrace her. And, separate from that harsh voice, there is the centered ME, who can experience the painful feelings of my parts and care for them."

The most important result of being free from your Critic is that you feel good about yourself. A natural sense of being valuable fills your consciousness. You walk taller and feel self-confident, capable, lovable, and good. You know you are worthwhile; you believe that you deserve appreciation and respect just for being yourself, not because you have done something to earn it. You understand that you don't have to accomplish something or be someone. It's not about the externals—you don't have to be smart, caring, or beautiful. You are valuable just for being you.

Many of our clients report that they learn to appreciate themselves. They feel good about their personal strengths, talents, and skills. They value their accomplishments and the ways they have grown. They appreciate what they have to offer to other people, and they see this reflected in how people respond to them.

When you are free of your Inner Critic, you accept yourself just as you are, including any limitations or problems. Your Inner Mentor helps you to be aware of your shortcomings without judgment. We are all works in progress. When you unconditionally accept yourself, it is easier to look at your issues because you don't judge yourself for them. You can hold up a mirror to look honestly at yourself because you don't have a Critic breathing down your neck. When changes are needed, creative solutions appear in intuitive ways. You have the inner support to take the risk to do things differently without any nagging self-judgment.

Most people find that, as they begin to change, they develop a palpable sense of confidence and inner trust. They walk forward without constantly looking over their shoulders or wasting time rehashing and regretting things they have said or done. They sense that their Inner Mentor is there to guide them in a kind, caring, accepting way. It becomes a real force in their lives. They develop a rhythm of knowing what to do and having the courage to follow through. This becomes a fall-back position that they can count on.

Since you can be guided by your Inner Mentor, you can move more fluidly toward becoming the person you want to be. Sometimes this does involve doing the things an Inner Critic might want you to do. You can work hard and produce excellence. You have integrity and care about other people; you are moderate in your appetites. You don't take unnecessary risks; you can appreciate tradition and follow convention when called for. The difference is that you can do all these things without needing to be pushed or judged by a Critic.

And you don't overdo them. You don't overwork or put yourself on a rigid diet, for example. You can choose to take these actions when a situation calls for them and only to the degree they are needed. When you make decisions in this way, they have an energy and an authenticity that put music in your step and draw other people toward your light. Your life is balanced, which makes it smoother and more fun.

Of course, this is an ideal picture we have just painted. As you transform your Critic parts, you will move toward this condition while not necessarily reaching it completely. After all, you don't have to be perfect.

More Inner Critic Material

In addition to the material in this book, there is an Inner Critic questionnaire and a profile application on our website (see Appendix B). By the time you read this, we may have additional applications and multimedia projects.

We know much more about Inner Critic work than we could put into this book, and we continue to study the Inner Critic. Here are a few of our books on the Inner Critic that are in the planning stages.

Therapist Book

There are a number of insights and processes that we haven't included in this book, either because they are primarily for therapists or because they are too technical for most non-therapists. These will be the basis for a separate book for therapists on Inner Critic work.

- Sometimes the exile that the Inner Critic is protecting is not the Criticized Child, but a different exile, which we call the Protected Child. We discuss how to distinguish between the two and how to heal the Protected Child.
- Sometimes it is useful to ask the Inner Critic (as well as the Criticized Child) to show you its origins in childhood.
- Sometimes there is a part that is attached to having the Inner Critic be as it is and doesn't want it to transform. We discuss how to work with such a part.
- We discuss how a therapist can help a client who has difficulty unblending from the Critic or the Criticized Child.
- We also discuss how a therapist can help a client who has difficulty unblending from a concerned part that is angry with the Critic.

Books on the Seven Types of Critics

We are planning books or booklets on most of the seven types of Critics. These will allow us to go into much more detail on each of them—how they operate, their motives, their origins, how to work with them, and exercises for evoking their Inner Champions.

Popular Inner Critic Book

We are planning a book based on clients' stories of their work with their Inner Critics. It won't require people to learn to do IFS on themselves and therefore should appeal to a wider audience than this book.

Criticism in Relationships

In Chapter 7, we just skimmed the surface of what can be said about the effect of criticism on relationships. A future book will cover this topic in more detail.

The Pattern System

In this book, we have explored the cluster of parts and healthy capacities that emerge in response to the Inner Critic and the issues around self-criticism and self-esteem. For years, Jay has been exploring the clusters of parts/capacities that are associated with many other psychological issues and dimensions. Each cluster has a similar structure to the one shown in this book. Jay has developed a personality system for understanding these clusters and how they relate to various dimensions of psychological experience and functioning. This *Pattern System* is introduced on our website and will be expanded and developed in future books.

Conclusion

IFS is a very powerful method for transforming your Inner Critic. We hope this book has made a significant difference in your internal landscape around self-esteem as well as in your life. We recommend that you use IFS for help with other psychological issues you may have.

Appendix A

Glossary

Accessing a Part Tuning in to a part experientially, through an image, an emotion, a body sensation, or internal dialogue, so you can work with the part using IFS.

Activation of a Part A part can become triggered by a situation or a person so that it influences your feelings and actions.

Blending The situation in which a part has taken over your consciousness, so that you feel its feelings, believe its attitudes are true, and act according to its impulses. Blending is a more extreme form of activation.

Burden A painful emotion or negative belief about yourself or the world, which a part has taken on as the result of a past harmful situation or relationship, usually from childhood.

Concerned Part A part that feels judgmental or angry toward the target part. When you are blended with a concerned part, you aren't in Self.

Conscious Blending The situation in which you choose to feel a part's emotions because doing so will be helpful in the IFS process. You are aware that you are blended and can unblend easily if necessary.

Criticized Child An exile who believes the judgments of the Inner Critic and feels ashamed, worthless, not valuable, guilty, self-doubting, or inadequate. It is both harmed and activated by the Critic.

Defender A protector that argues with people who judge you and that tries to prove that you are valuable and didn't do anything wrong.

Destroyer A type of Critic that makes pervasive attacks on your fundamental self-worth. It is deeply shaming and tells you that you shouldn't exist.

Exile A young child part that is carrying pain from the past.

Extreme Role A role that is dysfunctional or problematic because the part carries a burden from the past or because a protector is trying to protect an exile. An **extreme part** is a part that has an extreme role.

Guilt Tripper A type of Critic that attacks you for some specific action you took (or didn't take) in the past that was harmful to someone, especially someone you care about. It might also attack you for violating a deeply held value. It constantly makes you feel bad and will never forgive you.

Healthy Role A role that is the natural function of a part when it has no burdens. A **healthy part** is a part that has a healthy role.

Inner Champion An aspect of your Self that supports and encourages you and helps you feel good about yourself. It is the magic bullet for dealing with the negative impact of the Inner Critic.

Inner Controller A type of Critic that tries to control impulsive behavior, such as overeating, getting enraged, using drugs, or engaging in other addictions. It shames you after you binge or use. It is usually in a constant battle with an impulsive part.

Inner Critic A protector that judges you, demeans you, and pushes you to do things. It tends to make you feel bad about yourself.

Inner Defender A protector that tries to argue with the Critic and prove that you are worthwhile.

Inner Mentor The healthy version of the Critic. It encourages you to look at yourself with humility to see the ways in which you need to change how you operate in the world, and it helps you to make these changes in a supportive, encouraging way.

Judge A protector that judges other people, often to protect your Criticized Child.

Molder A type of Critic that tries to get you to fit a certain societal mold or act in a certain way that is based on your own family or cultural mores. It attacks you when you don't fit and praises you when you do.

Part A subpersonality, which has its own feelings, perceptions, beliefs, motivations, and memories.

Perfectionist A type of Critic that tries to get you to do everything perfectly. This part has very high standards for behavior, performance, and production. When you don't meet its standards, the Perfectionist attacks you by saying that your work or behavior isn't good enough.

Positive Intent All parts are playing their roles in an attempt to help you or protect you, even if the effect of the role is negative.

Protector A part that tries to block off pain that is arising inside you or to protect you from hurtful incidents or distressing relationships in your current life.

Reparenting The step in the IFS process in which the Self gives an exile what it needs to feel better or to change a harmful childhood situation.

Retrieval The step in the IFS process in which the Self takes an exile out of a harmful childhood situation and into a place where it can be safe and comfortable.

Role The job that a part performs to help you. It may be primarily internal, or it may involve the way the part interacts with people and acts in the world.

Self The core aspect of you that is your true self, your spiritual center. The Self is relaxed, open, and accepting of yourself and others. It is curious, compassionate, calm, and interested in connecting with other people and your parts.

Self-Leadership The situation in which your parts trust you, in Self, to make decisions and take action in your life.

Target Part The part you are focusing on to work with at the moment.

Taskmaster A type of Critic that tries to get you to work hard in order to be successful. It attacks you and tells you that you are lazy, stupid, or incompetent in order to motivate you. It often gets into a battle with a part that procrastinates in order to avoid work.

Trailhead A psychological issue that involves one or more parts. Following it can lead to healing.

Unblending Separating from a part that is blended with you so that you are in Self.

Unburdening The step in the IFS process in which the Self helps an exile to release its burdens through an internal ritual.

Underminer A type of Critic that tries to undermine your self-confidence and self-esteem so you won't take risks where you might fail. It may also try to prevent you from getting too big, powerful, or visible in order to avoid the threat of attack and rejection.

Witnessing The step in the IFS process in which the Self witnesses the childhood origin of a part's burdens.

Appendix B

Resources

IFS Therapists

If you want to find an IFS therapist to work with, consult the website of the Center for Self-Leadership, the official IFS organization, **www.selfleadership.org.** It contains a listing of IFS-certified therapists, which can be searched by geographical location. Some of these therapists, including ourselves, offer IFS sessions by telephone.

Inner Critic and IFS Classes and Groups

We teach classes for the general public on using IFS to work with the Inner Critic. They can be taken by telephone or in person in the San Francisco Bay Area. Each class is either a six-week course or a weekend workshop. We also offer classes in which people learn to use IFS for self-help and peer counseling, and classes on other psychological issues, such as overeating and procrastination.

We also offer ongoing IFS groups and classes, including ones over the telephone. In the future, Jay expects to offer a personal growth program lasting a year or more that will be based on IFS. See **www.personal-growth-programs.com** for more information and a schedule of classes and groups.

IFS Books by Jay and by Richard Schwartz, PhD

Self-Therapy: A Step-by-Step Guide to Creating Wholeness and Healing Your Inner Child Using IFS, by Jay Earley. Shows how to do IFS sessions on your own or with a partner. Also a manual of the IFS method that can be used by therapists. Bonnie has produced a card deck based on the illustrations in this book. See **www.personal-growth-programs.com.**

Introduction to the Internal Family System Model, by Richard Schwartz. A basic introduction to parts and IFS for clients and potential clients.

Internal Family Systems Therapy, by Richard Schwartz. The primary professional book on IFS and a must-read for therapists.

The Mosaic Mind: Empowering the Tormented Selves of Child Abuse Survivors, by Richard Schwartz and Regina Goulding. A professional book on using IFS with trauma, especially sexual abuse.

You Are the One You've Been Waiting For: Bringing Courageous Love to Intimate Relationships, by Richard Schwartz. A popular book providing an IFS perspective on intimate relationships.

To purchase Schwartz's books, visit the IFS store at **www.selfleadership.org.**

Companion Workbook

A compilation of all the exercises from this book that involve writing out answers. Download it for free from our website **www.personal-growth-programs.com.**

Illustrated Companion Book

A graphic support for "grokking" some of basic IFS and Inner Critic concepts. Contains illustrations from this book and some from *Self-Therapy* in large format and grouped for easy understanding.

Our Websites and Applications

Our IFS website, **www.personal-growth-programs.com,** contains quite a few popular and professional articles on IFS and its application to various psychological issues, and more are being added all the time. You can also sign up for our email list to receive future articles and notification of upcoming classes and groups.

Jay's personal website, **www.jayearley.com,** contains more of his writings and information about his practice, including his therapy groups.

Our other website, **www.psychemaps.com,** contains the Inner Critic Questionnaire and the Profiling Program for your Inner Critic and Inner Champion.

Appendix C

Help Sheets

You can refer to these Help Sheets to guide your steps while you are working on yourself.

They can also be used when you are facilitating for a partner.

Help Sheet 1: Getting to Know Your Inner Critic

P1. Accessing the Critic

If the Critic is not activated, imagine yourself in a situation in which it judges you.

Get an image of it and hear what it says to you.

P2. Unblending from the Criticized Child/Critic

Check to see if you are feeling bad about yourself or are believing that you are deficient.

Options for unblending:

- Remember that this is just a message from the Critic and not the truth.
- Listen to the Criticized Child's pain with compassion from Self.
- Ask the Criticized Child to go into a safe place so you can help both it and the Critic.

- Explain that you won't allow the Critic to attack it.
- Supply a nurturing aspect of Self to comfort the exile.
- Visualize the Critic in a room to provide a safe container for it.

P3. Unblending from the Inner Defender

Check to see how you feel toward the Critic right now.

If you feel compassionate, curious, etc., then you are in Self-leadership; move on to P4.

If you don't, then unblend from the Inner Defender as follows:

Ask if it would be willing to step aside (or relax) just for now so you can get to know the Critic part from an open place. Explain that doing this will help you to connect with the Critic and help it to change, and that you won't let the Critic take over and attack.

If the Defender is willing to step aside, check again to see how you feel toward the Critic, and repeat.

If it still won't step aside, ask what it is afraid would happen if it did, and reassure it about its fears.

P4. Finding Out about the Critic

Ask the Critic what it is trying to accomplish by judging you.
Ask what it is afraid would happen if it didn't.
Sense what exile it is trying to protect.

P5. Developing a Trusting Relationship with the Critic

You can foster trust by saying the following to the Critic (if true).

I understand what you are trying to do.

I appreciate your efforts on my behalf.

Help Sheet 2: Healing Your Criticized Child

2. Getting Permission to Work With Your Criticized Child

If necessary, ask the Critic to show you your Criticized Child.

Ask its permission to get to know the Child.

If it won't give permission, ask what it is afraid would happen if you accessed the Child.

Possibilities are:

The Child carries too much pain. Explain that you will stay in Self and get to know the Child, not dive into its pain.

There isn't any point in going into the pain. Explain that there is a point—you can heal the Child.

The Critic will have no role and will therefore be eliminated. Explain that the Critic can choose a new role in your psyche.

3. Getting to Know Your Criticized Child

E1: Accessing the Criticized Child

Sense its emotions, feel it in your body, or get an image of it.

E2: Unblending From Your Criticized Child

If you are blended with the Child:

Ask the Child to contain its feelings so you can be there for it.

Consciously separate from the Child and return to Self.

Get an image of the Child at a distance from you.

Do a centering/grounding meditation.

If the Child won't contain its feelings:

Ask it what it is afraid would happen if it did.

Explain that you really want to witness its feelings and story, but you need to be separate to do that.

Conscious blending: If you can tolerate it, allow yourself to feel some of the Child's pain.

E3: Unblending Concerned Parts

Check to see how you feel toward the Child.

If you aren't in Self or don't feel compassion, unblend from any concerned parts. They are usually afraid of your becoming overwhelmed by the Child's pain or the Child taking over.

Explain that you will stay in Self and not let the Child take over.

E4: Finding Out about Your Criticized Child

Ask: What do you feel? What makes you feel so bad about yourself?

E5: Developing a Trusting Relationship with Your Criticized Child

Let the Child know that you want to hear its story.

Communicate to it that you feel compassion and caring toward it.

Check to see if the Child can sense you, and notice if it is taking in your compassion.

4. Accessing and Witnessing Childhood Origins

Ask the Child to show you an image or a memory of when it learned to feel this way in childhood.

Ask the Child how this made it feel.

Check to make sure the Child has shown you everything it wants you to witness.

After witnessing, check to see if the Child believes that you understand how bad it was.

5. Reparenting Your Criticized Child

Bring yourself (as Self) into the childhood situation and ask the Child what it needs from you to heal it or to change what happened.

Protect it from being attacked or shamed.

Communicate to it your love, acceptance, and appreciation for it.

Check to see how the Child is responding to the reparenting.

If it can't sense you or isn't taking in your caring, ask why and work with that.

6: Retrieving Your Criticized Child

One of the things the Child may need is to be taken out of the childhood situation.

You can bring it into some place in your present life, your body, or an imaginary place.

7. Unburdening Your Criticized Child

Name the burdens (extreme feelings or beliefs) that the Child is carrying.

Ask the Child if it wants to release the burdens and if it is ready to do so.

If it doesn't want to, ask what it is afraid would happen if it let go of them. Then handle those fears.

How does the Child carry the burdens in or on its body?

What would the Child like to release the burdens to? (light, water, wind, earth, fire, or anything else)

Once the burdens are gone, notice what positive qualities or feelings arise in the Child.

8. Releasing the Critic

See if the Critic is aware of the transformation of the Child. If not, introduce the transformed Child to the Critic.

See if the Critic now realizes that its judgmental role is no longer necessary.

The Critic can choose a new role in your psyche.

Help Sheet 3: Transforming Your Critic

Introducing the Criticized Child to the Inner Critic

Access the Criticized Child.

Understand its pain, especially how it gets hurt by the Critic.

Introduce the Child to the Critic.

Ask the Critic if it realized it was hurting the Child.

Ask the Critic if it is ready to let go of its judgmental role.

If necessary, reassure it about any concerns it has about letting go.

Critic chooses new role.

Negotiating for Self-Leadership

Describe to the Critic what your capacities are as an adult in Self.

Explain to the Critic why the current life situations it is concerned about are not as dangerous as when you were young.

Tell it what you intend to do in these situations to handle them safely.

Ask the Critic to relax and let you lead in these situations.

If appropriate, explain to the Critic how it can aid you in a healthy way.

Made in the USA
San Bernardino, CA
21 December 2012